Surviving
The Real Mum's Guide to ∧Parenthood

About the Author

Jen Hogan lives in Dublin with her husband, Paul, and her seven children, Chloe, Adam, Jamie, Luke, Zach, Tobey and Noah. She is a blogger and freelance writer, and writes parenting articles for the *Irish Independent* and *Irish Examiner* and has contributed to articles in the *Irish Times*. She has also written for *Maternity and Infant* magazine, the *Ultimate Maternity Guide* and *Mums and Tots* magazine, and writes a regular column for *Easy Parenting* magazine. She often speaks about parenting issues on radio and television, including the *Ray D'Arcy Show*, Brenda O'Donohue's *Like Family, Today with Sean O'Rourke*, Newstalk, East Coast FM and the RTEjr parenting programme *Rearing to Go*.

Jen is passionate about all things parenting and about supporting mums and dads on the rollercoaster journey that is parenthood. You can follow the highs, lows and underwear battles of her parenting voyage on her blog, *Mama-tude*.

To link with Jen on social media:

Facebook: /mamatude7.ie
Twitter: @mama_tude
Instagram: @mama_tude
Website: mama-tude.com

The Real Mum's Guide to *Surviving* ∧ Parenthood

Jen Hogan

ORPEN PRESS

Published by
Orpen Press
Upper Floor, Unit K9
Greenogue Business Park
Rathcoole
Co. Dublin
Ireland

email: info@orpenpress.com
www.orpenpress.com

Paperback ISBN 978-1-78605-032-8
ePub ISBN 978-1-78605-033-5
Kindle ISBN 978-1-78605-034-2
PDF ISBN 978-1-78605-035-9

Printed in Dublin by SPRINTprint Ltd

For Paul, Chloe, Adam, Jamie, Luke, Zach, Tobey and Noah.
And for the four I never held in my arms, but hold always in my heart.

Acknowledgements

Thank you:

To Orpen Press for taking a chance on me and for allowing me to see a dream realised. To Gerry, Sam, Gráinne and all those behind the scenes for all your hard work and fabulously approachable manner. To my wonderful editor, Eileen, for your support and patience with my novice author ways and for never expressing the slightest bit of shock at my longwinded ramblings via email at 4 a.m. and for managing to decipher exactly what it was that I was asking, in the midst of it all.

To my wonderful husband, Paul, my partner in crime, for being my rock and fall guy.

To my own 'Magnificent Seven' for being my teachers and for continuing to wrong-foot me, just when I thought I had this parenting lark sussed. For asking me, on repeat, 'Are you done yet? Are you done yet?', every step of the way, reminding me that I am always a parent, no matter how pressing the engagement. To my beautiful right-hand woman, Chloe, the first of the brood – the one who made me 'Mum'. To my gorgeous boys for always being there with hugs and for teaching me about priorities, and that the wearing of underwear is not necessarily one.

To my mum and dad, sisters, extended family and friends for all of your encouragement and support. To my in-laws for sharing in the excitement and always championing me, and to Mary and Terry for traipsing to ours on a regular basis to help with homework, school collections and kung fu runs so that I could sometimes write in daylight hours. To Pamela for prodding and never allowing me to give up when I was sorely tempted.

Acknowledgements

To Paula who has always been there.

To my work colleagues and friends for your terrific support in so many regards.

To the Irish Parenting Bloggers, my virtual support network, who have helped me to appreciate that there is no such thing as a perfect parent. Imperfectly parenting is the way forward – as is winging it sometimes and hoping for the best.

To the amazing *Mama-tude* readers, without whom there would be no book. Thank you for reading and sharing and chatting and messaging and for giving me the confidence to do this.

And to you the reader – thank you so very much for reading.

CONTENTS

Contents

Contents

1

IN THE BEGINNING

In the beginning, there was a stick – and somewhere between one and three minutes later (depending on sensitivity), that stick told the story of what was to come. Two pink lines later and the confirmation was there. Not (chances are) that you accepted the first result, but after twenty-five more tests, all showing the same tell-tale pink lines, you begin to finally acknowledge that there is a distinct possibility you may be pregnant. And so begins the wonderful journey to parenthood, filled with a myriad of emotions, plenty of nausea, excessive weight gain and piles for good measure.

Over the years pregnancy tests have featured heavily in my life, but the first time I saw those two lines – which indicated life as I knew it was about to change forever – was in the bathroom at work. I should be honest, it's not a place I'd recommend taking such an important test, as it's pretty difficult trying to remain composed in front of colleagues when your heart is pounding and you're silently screaming 'OH MY GOD, OH MY GOD' in your head. Hindsight, however, is a wonderful thing, and so with it lacking I took the test. Gobsmacked by the result, I did what any sane person would do: I returned to my office, made my excuses and headed off to the chemist, pee-covered stick in my pocket, to confirm with the pharmacist my suspicions – that the test was faulty.

This was a much-wanted baby and as biology had been my forte at school it really shouldn't have come as such a shock to be pregnant in the first place, but the simple irony of the overwhelming feelings I had about the fact that I was growing a new life were indicative of the emotional rollercoaster ahead. To this day, pregnancy and motherhood have been the greatest privileges ever bestowed on me. I'm lucky enough to have had the experience of both a fair few times, and as my parenting journey started with pregnancy so did my parenting life lessons.

I learned that every pregnancy is different and that old wives' tales are really just that and have no bearing on the sex of your unborn child. I discovered that, in spite of knowing this fact, countless times over I would still analyse my symptoms accordingly and neurotically in an attempt to predict the gender of the baby on board. I learned that having an ability to leave your dignity at the door, sometimes at least, was a huge asset. I also sadly learned that pregnancy does not guarantee a baby.

But probably the biggest thing I learned over the course of my pregnancies was the amazing resilience of women. Whether it's an additional risk pregnancy or a particularly symptomatic one, us women tend to do the necessary, endure the required and keep going. Mother Nature is a crafty one. She cleverly makes us forget the more challenging aspects once we set eyes on our beloved babies – until we pee on another stick and see two lines again that is.

In spite of the ups and downs of pregnancy, I have to admit I love it. I love the excitement, I love the closeness and I'm still very much in awe of the whole miracle that is 'life'. As for the *more* than nine event-filled months involved, knowing what to expect is a huge help. And so, moving on, here are some of the things you can expect during pregnancy: some pleasant and some slightly more 'challenging', but as they say forewarned is forearmed.

MORNING SICKNESS

Morning sickness is perhaps the most inaccurately named sickness of all time. Although it affects the majority of pregnant women to some degree, I managed to escape it on the pregnancies of my first and fourth children. Incidentally, the babies were different sexes so any myths surrounding gender-based morning sickness prevalence can be dispelled now.

The first time around, an appetite of impressive magnitude took hold instead. Not only did I want to eat incessantly, I wanted to eat every type of food imaginable, and amongst many other things, this almost vegetarian started to crave meat. My appetite became a source of amusement for all who knew me and few were brave enough to leave their dinners or desserts in my line of vision.

I assumed things would follow a similar pattern when I was pregnant with my second child. However, around the six-week mark I started to feel queasy. Queasiness progressed very quickly to a second viewing of everything I ate. I initially confused it with a stomach bug because – very unlike its name – the sickness lasted all day. As the days passed, it became obvious that no one else in the house was ill and this special time spent with my head down the toilet was reserved just for me.

Until I experienced it myself, I never really appreciated how restrictive and all-consuming morning sickness could be. Even the commute to work was a challenge. While I got used to working the green-tinged look, I couldn't get used to the need to hop off the bus at random stops for fear of throwing up on board and the amount of extra time that my commute took as a result.

Many people like to keep news of their pregnancy a secret until at least the twelve-week mark, but if you're struggling with morning sickness then it's definitely worth letting your boss and maybe some sympathetic colleagues know. Diet cola, boiled sweets and ice pops were my saviour during those weeks. I kept a supply on my desk, in my handbag and in my freezer. Eating small bland snacks and frequent meals, even if I didn't feel much like it at the time, was essential because hunger made the nausea worse.

In my case morning sickness lasted beyond the promised twelve-week mark but it did greatly improve by week sixteen. I began to enjoy my food again (a little too much if truth be told) and smells that once triggered feelings of nausea became less of an issue. My time-keeping at work hugely improved too.

Damned If You Do, Damned If You Don't

The thing about morning sickness is the feeling that you're damned if you do have it and damned if you don't. It has been suggested that morning sickness is generally a sign of a well-progressing pregnancy. Its absence the first time didn't cause me any great concern as I had no previous pregnancies to compare it with. But when it failed to put in an appearance during the pregnancy of my fourth child, a sense of panic set in.

By this stage I had sadly experienced two miscarriages and on both occasions had experienced no morning sickness. Although my first morning-sickness-free pregnancy had resulted in a healthy bouncing baby girl, nothing could alleviate my sense of fear that something was going to go wrong with baby number four. I felt too well. I looked too well (purely in a non-green-tinged kind of way). I was sure I was in trouble.

I was wrong and my perfect baby boy arrived into the world several months later, barely in time for Christmas. He was just giving me an easy time of it and this experienced mum was reminded once again how different every pregnancy is.

HORMONES

Ladies, if you think PMT is a curse, you ain't seen nothing yet. Prior to pregnancy, I liked to think of myself as a fairly non-confrontational type of gal. Pragmatic, diplomatic, rational even, are all words that might have been used to describe me in that period of my life, long, long ago, before I ever experienced pregnancy. But a shadow was cast upon me and my tongue no longer remained under my control. Things and people that I found mildly irritating before the hormonal tsunami that engulfed me became less mildly so. At one stage I found myself sitting alone in the office at lunchtime, just to avoid a certain colleague with an opinion on everything and a blurred and rather fantastically obscured view of her own family. I couldn't trust myself not to make everything that little bit clearer for her.

No one was safe; I developed an opinion on everything and sat on the fence about nothing so this self-imposed lunchtime solitary confinement continued in the interest of good post-pregnancy colleague relations. When I wasn't agitated by others breathing, I cried. I cried because Sonia in *Eastenders* gave birth to a baby girl and gave her the name I intended for my baby (my husband vetoed the name once Sonia used it). I cried at soap break-ups. I cried because I gained a stone and a half in four weeks. I cried because I couldn't fit behind the wheel of my car and I cried because I ran out of digestive biscuits.

Civility did return to me after my baby was born and my baby girl did, in the end, receive my name of choice, when my husband immediately relented following the whole childbirth spectacle. The tendency to burst into tears stuck around though. I've come to the conclusion that was nature's way of preparing me for what was to come. Once your baby is born, your perspective changes forever and you can never view the world in the same way again.

Although hormonal changes are a very natural part of pregnancy, it's important to keep an eye on any persistent, intensifying mood swings or feelings of anxiety. Perinatal anxiety and depression can occur and it's always best to speak with your doctor if you're concerned about how you're feeling.

EVERYONE HAS AN OPINION

Pregnancy is a time of wonderful public empathy – a smile from a stranger who catches a glimpse of your growing belly, a nod from a neighbour who mentions the exciting times to come and a reassuring comment from a fellow mum-to-be with a similar-sized tummy, who happens to be five months further along than you, but still earnestly and sincerely tells you how 'neat' you are.

It's also a time when the world and its sister seem to have an opinion on what you should or shouldn't do, and on what you should or shouldn't expect. Being subject to public scrutiny of the familial, or other, kind is not a concept most of us are receptive to but it doesn't seem to stop the 'helpful' suggestions flooding in.

While unsolicited advice might not always be welcome, it is generally well intended as pregnancy is a time of great excitement for most people. The difficult part to handle is when your food choices and activity levels are questioned by an older generation who did things quite differently. 'It didn't do me any harm' is usually the argument of choice here. Personally, I found the best way of avoiding an argument or causing offence was to say that I just couldn't go against the latest medical advice. 'There must be a reason for it', I'd always add.

In fairness, it can be difficult for a generation who has already successfully navigated pregnancy and raised a family to understand why we do things differently now, but, to this day, as I regularly point out, things change so frequently that advice I followed for my first child was already outdated by my fourth, never mind my seventh.

So in the midst of your pregnancy, prepare yourself to hear how you shouldn't raise your arms above your head, how heartburn means your baby has lots of hair, and how the shape of your bump and the manner in which you're carrying apparently reveals the gender; those brave enough might even comment on its impressive size and ask if you're sure there's not twins or triplets in there. This is a good time to practise that breathing you learned in antenatal classes.

For reassurance, can I add that bumps do indeed come in many varied shapes and sizes, and all of mine were enormous. Helpful comments of 'you'll never lose all that weight' aside, baby was healthy, though on the large side, and no hidden sibling was ever found alongside any singleton in my uterus.

TOILET TIME

The bathroom is a room in which you'll spend more and more time over the course of your pregnancy. When morning sickness has passed and the inconvenience of constant urination eases (for a time), your toilet trips will be replaced with back-soothing relaxing baths and refreshing showers. You'll also possibly spend a fair bit of time there dealing with constipation and piles – another of nature's little jokes. Get ready to leave your dignity at the door of the chemist, this time as you discuss solutions with your pharmacist for a sluggish digestive system and haemorrhoids, such is the glamourous life of a pregnant lady.

Thankfully there are things that can be taken to encourage 'movement' if it happens, but prevention is definitely better than cure, so try to stay hydrated, do some moderate exercise and include plenty of fibre in your diet.

TIREDNESS

Growing a person is hard work and utterly exhausting. When increasing levels of progesterone are added to the equation, it's no surprise that you might well find yourself falling asleep anywhere and everywhere. Tiredness wasn't a symptom of pregnancy that I was prepared for, assuming all exhaustion was reserved for the third trimester when a burgeoning bump added to your load, so that one really caught me off guard. There's not really anything you can do here except rest when the opportunity presents itself, which is very difficult if you have other children. It will pass over by the second trimester and return in a different form by the third trimester, but at least by that stage you'll feel fully justified in collapsing to the floor in exhaustion having mounted a flight of stairs.

Of course, there are lots of wonderful things about pregnancy too, which are often forgotten about when dealing with the variety of more unpleasant side effects and the adjustment to your changing body and impending changing role.

BABY KICKS

Definitely one of the most exciting times during your pregnancy is the first and subsequent times that you feel your little baby kick. When to expect this often depends on whether or not it's your first pregnancy and/or the position of your placenta. On my first child, I didn't feel any movement until after twenty weeks, while I felt fluttering by fourteen weeks on child two. Child four had a placenta cushioning his kicks and so made for a very stressful pregnancy, as I worried about the lack of reassuring movement.

Starting as a bubble-like feeling, it's not long before you'll become very aware of baby's movement and even eventually notice typical sleeping patterns. As well as a wonderful reminder that you're not alone and an exciting hint of what's to come, baby's kicks are a fantastic way of knowing how baby is.

If you notice a slowdown in movements, try a very cold drink or a change in position. If things don't change contact your doctor. Never worry that you might be overreacting. It's always better to err on the side of caution and the doctors and midwives would prefer to have the opportunity to confirm all is well.

One thing to remember is that it is *not* true that baby movements slow down as you get closer to labour, so never delay in seeking medical attention.

SCAN PHOTOS

Baby's first picture and your real and true confirmation that you're not just suffering from a bad case of indigestion – scan pictures have come a long way from the grainy images of years ago. Some hospitals even incorporate 3D and 4D images as part of their routine scans these days. The clarity is pretty amazing and if you have other children you can sometimes even spot sibling similarities from quite an early stage.

When you have a scan and how many you'll have depends on many things: from the hospital or facility you're attending; to any concerns surrounding your pregnancy or baby's position, health and size; location of the placenta; etc. Some hospitals offer dating scans at around twelve weeks and an anomaly scan is usually carried out somewhere between eighteen and twenty-two weeks.

While it's wonderful to get a close-up of baby in the womb, anomaly scans of course serve a purpose. During the scan the position of the placenta and the amount of amniotic fluid is measured.

Limb, head and stomach measurements are also taken and plotted to confirm the expected delivery date. The anatomical structure of the baby and various organs are examined and the person carrying out the ultrasound will look for indications of any abnormalities. While obvious structural abnormalities may be seen, not all conditions can or will be picked up by the scan, but any 'soft markers' which may possibly indicate a problem will be discussed with you. From my own perspective, I was lucky that a very treatable condition was picked up during one of my babies' scans. Throughout his pregnancy, I was scanned frequently to monitor the condition and a paediatrician was present at his birth.

Some hospitals give you the option of finding out the gender and that's obviously a very personal decision. I chose never to find out but be warned that if you follow this course you'll need to remind the sonographer/midwife/obstetrician at every appointment that you don't want to know. Wanting a 'surprise' puts you in the minority nowadays it seems and you'll find some medics need more work than others on their poker faces.

GLOWING LOCKS AND SKIN – AND OTHER THINGS

While it's not a guarantee, many women will find that their hair, skin and nails look better than ever during pregnancy. Thanks to pregnancy hormones, you'll lose less hair than usual, which makes your luscious locks look thicker and healthier. In addition to hormones, an increased blood volume means your skin will appear brighter and (hopefully) positively radiant, while your nails grow faster than ever before.

Also growing at an impressive rate are your boobs. This generally starts very early on and you may well need to change bra size several times over the course of the pregnancy. How welcome a change this is depends on the individual, but one thing that cannot but be appreciated is that short period of time during the pregnancy when, except for the difficulty of sensitive nipples, you could go bra-less if you chose and resemble a lady who has had a boob job: impressive in size, stature and position without any added silicone. Oh, if only it lasted ….

ANTENATAL AND BREASTFEEDING CLASSES

These are really important classes to attend and my own experience was to find them hugely enjoyable. In addition to learning coping techniques for labour and new skills for after baby's birth, they are a wonderful way to meet other women at a similar stage of pregnancy and maybe get some answers to questions you may have.

What happens directly after baby's birth – from skin-to-skin contact, to baby potentially needing to go to the Special Care Baby Unit, to feeding your baby – are all discussed in detail at the classes. The explanation of the midwife to the room 'that breasts have a purpose – even if you daddies like to play with the empties' still makes me laugh to this day.

However, antenatal classes are not just for first-time mums. Refresher classes are an option for second and subsequent mums who might like a reminder about what's involved or who may be hoping for a vaginal birth after a previous C-section.

The classes are an invaluable resource, helping to take some of the mystery and possible fear out of what lies ahead. In many cases the classes also involve a trip to the labour ward, which was notably absent of the instruments of torture I had conjured up in my head. Seeing the bright and welcoming surroundings was very reassuring ahead of D-Day and made me feel a lot calmer about everything.

HOSPITAL BAG

Us ladies have many strengths, but packing lightly is not necessarily one of them. How long a mother can expect to stay in hospital largely depends on the type of birth she has and how she and baby are afterwards. Typically, there is very little space to store your belongings while at hospital, so it's best to bring only the necessities and to remember that additional requirements can be brought later by visiting family or friends.

Essential things to include in your hospital bag are:
For you:

- Your maternity file (if you keep it with you)
- An old nightshirt for giving birth in
- Three pairs of pyjamas, ideally ones that button down (for ease of access for breastfeeding)
- Dressing gown
- Slippers
- Flip-flops for the shower
- Three dark towels
- Maternity pads, with no plastic backing (at least two packets)
- Six to ten pairs of high-waisted big dark knickers (I found the maternity pads didn't sit as well in the disposable ones and proper knickers felt more secure)
- Comfortable wire-free nursing bras – your boobs can feel pretty tender when your milk comes in
- Breast pads
- Toiletries bag, with tooth brush, shampoo, shower cap, etc.
- Loose/maternity clothing to wear going home
- Phone charger
- Books or magazines

For baby (all clothes, towels and sheets should be pre-washed):

- Six long-sleeved babygros
- Six baby vests
- Cardigan
- Baby hat
- Scratch mitts
- Bibs or muslin cloths
- Baby towel
- Cotton wool
- Petroleum jelly
- Newborn nappies
- Nappy bags

- Two baby blankets
- Three Moses-basket-sized sheets

It's quite likely you'll need more maternity pads, baby nappies and possibly even pyjamas brought into you during your stay at hospital, so it's a good idea to have these purchased and waiting at home, at the ready.

AND SO ON TO THE EXIT ROUTE ...

All good things must come to an end and eventually, when it's time for baby to leave the safe confines of your womb and meet his or her awaiting and adoring public, the exit route takes one of two options. Ideals aside, childbirth, like pregnancy, can be incredibly unpredictable and it's important to remember that the best-laid plans can still go awry.

Birth choices are an immensely personal thing and what one woman aims for can be completely different to another woman's hopes. The safety of mum and baby is of course the most important thing but don't be afraid to cut yourself a little slack if you find yourself feeling disappointed that things didn't turn out the way you had planned.

Childbirth is a huge event, whatever shape it takes. Having experienced both vaginal births and C-sections, I can honestly say that neither is the easier option. Both are very different, with different recoveries and different periods of pain, but they both definitely involve 'giving birth' – even the less traditional route.

Eviction Time

Only 5 per cent of babies actually arrive on their due dates – and yet we as mums put so much emphasis on it, counting down the weeks and days, especially towards the end when a big bump and accompanying waddle makes everything just seem like so much effort. It's not uncommon for due dates to come and go without any sign of baby making an entrance to the world while endless excited texts and calls can make you feel under pressure to 'perform'.

If baby seems far too comfy and reluctant to evacuate their cosy surroundings, there are one or two things you can do that might help things along. Exercise is a great place to start. A good walk could get things moving. Bouncing on a gym ball is another good idea. Not only is the gym ball incredibly comfortable, it has the added bonus of correcting your posture while the bouncing motion encourages baby further down into your pelvis.

A hot curry or spicy food is another rumoured way to trigger labour. Of course there is always the risk that instead of having a baby afterwards you end up with a bad case of heartburn. Castor oil is best avoided for equally unpleasant reasons. Nausea and diarrhoea are the most likely outcomes here.

It might be difficult to manage during late pregnancy, or even muster up the enthusiasm for it, but having sex may actually trigger labour. Not only does sex result in the release of oxytocin, which can cause contractions, but semen actually contains prostaglandins, which are used in the induction process.

Of course all best efforts and amorous attempts to bring baby into the world may not make a difference and eager parents may just have to wait patiently until baby is ready to meet their audience. Consider it further preparation for what lies ahead. Patience is a virtue, of which you'll need lots over the coming years.

Am I in Labour?

First-time mums, in particular, often worry how they'll know if they're really in labour. I won't lie: labour is hard work and it hurts – but not in the Hollywood-type way, where one minute a glamourous actress is going about her business and the next minute she clutches her stomach in agony and declares with absolute certainty, 'this is it!'

Every woman is different and every labour is different but the likelihood is that the build-up to your labour will be a bit more gradual than in the movies. Losing the mucous plug, or 'the bloody show', is sometimes the first sign that things are about to get started – but not always. Sometimes the plug comes away hours before labour starts. Sometimes it's days. Sometimes it's even weeks. Bleeding and a bloody show are different though. A bloody show is blood-stained mucous. Bleeding, on the other hand, should always be checked by the hospital.

Labour pains can start out as period-like cramps in either your stomach or back. It's easy to confuse them with 'Braxton Hicks'. Braxton Hicks are practice contractions or tightenings, which shouldn't be painful though you'll often be very aware of them. Labour pains hurt.

If you're in labour, what started as period-like pains will progress in terms of intensity, duration and frequency. If you can talk and go about your business, largely as normal, it's unlikely that you're in labour – yet. Time your contractions, time the interval between them and measure your own ability to cope. Call the labour ward and speak to a midwife for guidance. Don't struggle unnecessarily. If you're finding things particularly hard-going, go in. Everyone is different and every experience is different.

Our natural inclination when we're in pain is to tense up, but the breathing exercises practised in antenatal classes can really help with the pain, and to cope with the fear. Try to breathe slowly and deeply as contractions come and remind yourself that they will peak and pass. If you can help your body to relax it will take the edge off the pain and it will help you to keep calm. If your birth partner is with you, ask them to help you by breathing with you.

For some women, their waters break ahead of going into labour. For others, it happens while in labour. And for other women, their waters will be broken by the person delivering their baby. Often a woman's contractions will intensify once her waters have gone – but again, not always. Regardless of whether or not your contractions have started, if you think your waters have broken you need to seek medical advice. The baby is at risk of infection if they are without the sterile amniotic fluid environment for too long.

Labour tends to be shorter on subsequent pregnancies – something to be mindful of in terms of childcare arrangements for older children and the amount of time to allow before heading to the hospital. It can also take a different form. My waters broke in the middle of the night, without warning, on child number five (who was supposed to be an elective C-section). There were no pains ahead of this happening, and at the time just a slightly frazzled husband who was keen to get me to the hospital as quickly as possible and was a little perturbed by my insistence that 'I'd just put on a bit of lippy first.'

If you had a previous difficult experience, try not to worry. Every labour is different and it's far from a foregone conclusion that difficulties you may have encountered first time around will prove to be the case again.

Vaginal Birth

Vaginal births can be spontaneous or induced. Spontaneous, assuming adequate gestation, is often most people's preferred choice. The excitement of the unknown, the rumoured additional pain associated with induction and the naturalness of baby arriving when baby is allegedly ready means that most of us, first time around anyway, are happy enough to wait for nature to take its course.

There are times, however, when induction is necessary. Most hospitals have a policy of not allowing women to go past 42 weeks of pregnancy. At this stage of pregnancy there is a worry that the placenta is becoming old and might not function as well as it should. Other medical reasons a woman might have her labour induced include blood pressure issues, pre-eclampsia and foetal difficulties.

Once a woman is in established labour, she will generally be transferred to the labour ward, where, if so desired, she can avail of the by now infamous epidural. This, of course, is assuming an anaesthesiologist is available to administer one. Many other forms of pain relief, both natural and medical, are also available.

Some maternity hospitals have a birthing pool where the natural soothing effects of water can be used to help manage the pain. Entonox, commonly referred to as 'gas and air', is another option which can help to take the edge off labour pain, while pethidine is a morphine-like form of pain relief administered by intra-muscular injection. Because pethidine can make baby drowsy it's usually not given too close to delivery.

A TENS machine, which is a small battery-operated device, is another popular form of pain relief, particularly in early labour. Sticky pads are applied to your back and connected by leads to a handheld controller. The machine releases mild electrical currents which prevent pain signals from reaching your brain and stimulate your body to release endorphins.

Hypnobirthing, meanwhile, is growing in popularity as a natural method of coping with labour through mind-calming techniques which in turn encourage your body to relax. It's not, however, something that you can just decide upon at the time of delivery. Hypnobirthing involves practice for both mum and her birth partner in the months and weeks before labour.

Opting for pain relief, or not, is as individual as the mum-to-be. Keeping an open mind and 'seeing how you go' is the best position to take and the one most likely to help you reconcile with the realities of labour and childbirth.

My Own Vaginal Births

My first vaginal birth involved an induction after an ongoing difficulty with rising blood pressure and progressive swelling, which saw me resemble the Michelin Man more and more as the days passed. I had thought I was just having a check-up that day and was taken aback by the consultant's suggestion that it was time to get things moving.

Two doses of prostaglandin gel were enough to get the labour started. I had polyhydramnios (excessive levels of amniotic fluid) during the pregnancy and when my waters broke I got to see exactly what this meant. My labour progressed quickly and I was moved to the labour ward. After much pleading, an anaesthesiologist was called to administer an epidural. I had no desire to have a drug-free birth and when that epidural kicked in the world seemed a much happier place. Twenty minutes later, my daughter was born.

My entire labour lasted two hours from start to finish and as wonderful as that sounds in theory, it was quite a scary experience as there was no break between contractions and at the time I didn't realise it would be over in two hours. The high I felt at her birth, however, was like nothing I had ever experienced before. I was also very surprised to see I had given birth to a baby girl, having been totally convinced I had a baby boy on board. She was shocked by the experience and spent a few days in an incubator in the Special Care Baby Unit. But she was perfect and I was head over heels in love with this amazing little human that I had created (with a little help) – and so it began.

Vaginal birth number two was a different experience. After many false starts, baby decided to leave me waiting and I went several days overdue before he decided to arrive in a frantic manner, just like his sister.

After arriving at the maternity hospital in pain, I was informed that I was not in labour. I was told to return in four days when I would be induced. Minutes later, on the car journey home my waters broke in equally spectacular style to the first time (again I had polyhydramnios) and my husband, in a panic, turned the car around and made his way back to the hospital, terrified at the possibility that he might have to deliver the baby himself. Once at the hospital we made our way to the labour ward again and I apologised to everyone I passed for the trail of water I was leaving behind as I walked. In between the agony of contractions, I sought out someone to get a mop in case of a slippage.

Once examined, I was told that I was not dilating but as my waters had gone they would keep me in. Having been here before I knew my child's birth was imminent and asked for an epidural but none was forthcoming. Ten minutes later I shouted that I needed to push. An unconvinced midwife muttered something about me being a drama queen and reluctantly examined me. Seconds later she called for assistance as my baby's head crowned. Fear took hold as I realised that I was going to need to deliver this baby without pain relief. Moments later my son entered the world to the sound of a midwife telling me that I was defying the laws of obstetrics. This time it was my turn to be in shock. Natural childbirth had never featured in my plan but my son was here, healthy and safe. Once again, my gender prediction was inaccurate and my conviction that I was expecting a girl was proven wrong. It's just as well I'm not a betting woman.

Caesarean Sections

There are a lot of common misconceptions about C-sections. One is that they are an easier option. Another is that a woman might choose one if she is 'too posh to push'. There also seems to be confusion about the number of C-sections that a woman can have. A caesarean section is major abdominal surgery and most definitely is not an easy option. The pain at the time of delivery might be deferred but the recovery is longer and the restrictions are more.

A planned or elective caesarean section is, as the name suggests, a much calmer affair than an emergency caesarean section, where the emphasis is on getting baby delivered as quickly as possible, because baby is in difficulty.

An elective C-section is often scheduled ahead of the due date and reasons might include previous C-sections, position of the baby, maternal or foetal health issues, position of the placenta or multiple pregnancy. With an elective section, you will generally be asked to fast for a certain period of time beforehand. Ahead of the procedure, you will be shaved and any blind attempts you made to do the job yourself will be put right.

A birth partner can join you for the delivery, provided you are awake for the procedure. Anaesthesia will be administered to your spine and a catheter inserted. Anti-nausea medication will be given if you feel sick and a screen erected in front of you, so you won't see what's going on. Your birth partner sits at your head, the doctor confirms that you are numb and then they begin.

There is no pain during the delivery and it only takes minutes. There is a sensation of tugging and a little pressure to help baby into the world. Baby is then lifted over the screen for you to see and the sex revealed, if you didn't already know. Paediatricians are in the theatre at the time of delivery and they check baby over. Once all is well, you can have your cuddles.

It takes longer to stitch you up afterwards, but chances are you'll be on such a high you'll barely notice the time passing. At this stage, you will be transferred to the recovery room for plenty of skin-to-skin contact and you can feed your baby.

My C-Section Experiences

Five of my births have been by caesarean section, two of which were categorised as emergency C-sections. The reality in my case was that they were emergency sections because I went into labour ahead of my scheduled C-sections. Thankfully, there was no drama involved, except the one caused at home by baby number six, who chose to enter the world three weeks early and on the day of his sister's twelfth birthday. Mammy guilt was hardest thing to cope with here as I spent the day in hospital away from my firstborn.

The one thing I did find with my elective C-sections, which is probably true of any planned surgery, is that nerves kicked in ahead of the big day. The surgery itself was fine, though the spinal block always made me sick and I worried each time that my husband wouldn't arrive into theatre in time for the birth. Sure enough, he made it on each occasion, decked out in his very fetching surgical attire.

It's a surreal feeling when you see your baby lifted up over the screen. There has been no pain, just pressure, and then you hear this tiny person announce his or her arrival to the world and you just can't see them quickly enough. Skin-to-skin is now practised with C-section babies and it's wonderful to get to hold your little one so soon.

My husband took care of my babies while I was sewn up after surgery and I was reunited with baby again in the recovery room where I could breastfeed. The catheter stays in place for twenty-four hours and pain medication is kept topped up. It's hard not being allowed to eat or drink anything, except ice-cubes, until the next day and the morphine made me feel very itchy.

Luckily, I found my fifth C-section no more difficult to recover from than the first, but that may have been pure luck – and if that's the case I'm so glad luck was on my side as with so many children to take care of and no family support close by I needed to be back on my feet as quickly as possible.

Many people are surprised by the number of C-sections I've had, and while I frequently joke that they should have put a zipper in I was advised by my obstetrician that the number of caesarean sections a person can have varies from woman to woman. It depends largely on her recovery, scar tissue and how her womb heals. There is no one number that fits all.

RECOVERING FROM CHILDBIRTH

Recovery from childbirth can differ significantly, depending on whether the birth was vaginal or a C-section. Either way, it is important to remember that your body has been through a huge ordeal and you need to rest up and give yourself a chance to heal.

If you have had a vaginal delivery and required stitches, you may find it difficult to go to the toilet in the days following. Urination can sting, so pouring warm water over the area as you pee can help to ease the pain – and yes, your contortionist abilities might well be tested.

A bowel movement can be even more scary, as fear takes hold that you might burst your stitches. Holding a clean sanitary towel against your perineum (the area between your vagina and your anus) as your bowels open can help you to feel more comfortable and secure. It's very important to keep your stitches clean so change your pad regularly, and always make sure to dry your perineum after bathing.

A caesarean section naturally requires a longer recovery period, as it is major abdominal surgery and the wound requires particular care to prevent infection. In the days following a C-section, laughing, coughing or sneezing can be uncomfortable. Lying on your side can invoke a 'dragging' sensation, so it might be more comfortable to sleep on your back.

The catheter generally stays in place for approximately twenty-four hours, as you won't have any feeling in your legs for a period after delivery. It can feel a little difficult to pee afterwards. Drinking plenty can increase the urge and help a little, but the sensation of trying to 'let go' can feel strange. Bowel movements can also be very uncomfortable as a result of internal trauma so plenty of fluids and fibre are in order to help assist with this.

Getting up on your feet as soon as possible is very important but never lift anything heavier than your baby. The one piece of advice I would give to anyone who has had a C-section is to always stay on top of your pain medication in the days that follow. Don't make the mistake of thinking you're fine. You feel fine because of the pain relief. If that wears off it can take a while to build back up the cumulative effect, as I learned the hard way.

When you return home, don't overestimate your abilities. I made the mistake of thinking I could walk to my children's school when my baby was just eight days old. While I survived the relatively short walk there, I hobbled home in agony as my healing wound became very sore thanks to my over-exertion.

If the wound becomes sore, raised or hot, or oozes at any stage, seek medical advice; likewise if you find yourself with a temperature. Comfortable loose clothing and underwear are essential as your wound heals. High waists are definitely preferable so don't discard the maternity clothes too early.

The key is to take it as easy as you can and allow yourself time to recover. Don't be tempted to hurry things along – you risk setting yourself back further in the long run. Take advantage of the recovery time to rest, recuperate and get to know the new little person in your life. In the grand scheme of things, it's a short enough period of time.

MISCARRIAGE

Sometimes described as a taboo, miscarriage is one of the aspects of pregnancy that we never really want to talk about, or consider – unless we've sadly been there. It's estimated that roughly one in four pregnancies end in miscarriage, though it has been suggested that the rate may well be higher taking into account the fact that many miscarriages occur before a woman even knows she is pregnant. With statistics like this, it's not surprising that most of us will know someone who has been affected by miscarriage, or maybe will have been through it ourselves. Even armed with the numbers, if it happens to you it can be one of the saddest and loneliest times. A dream shattered, a heart broken, a baby lost.

I never expected to be the one in four. I never thought it could happen to me, and absolutely nothing could have prepared me for the first time. Sitting at home as my toddler daughter dozed in her cot, I felt something was wrong. I was young, just over three months pregnant and had experienced no sickness – but it wasn't that. I was never sick during my first pregnancy either, so I assumed this was the way things rolled.

I was due to have my first scan two days later and I was really looking forward to it. But something just didn't feel right. I paused the programme I was watching and went to the bathroom. My world began to unravel.

I made a phone call to my husband. His colleague picked up the phone and she congratulated me on my news. We were past the three-month mark. He had told everyone just the week before that he was to be a dad again. My sobbed response made her call my husband quickly.

'I'm bleeding', I told him. 'I think I'm losing the baby.'

I rushed to the hospital, in the naive belief that they could do something. That they could put a stitch in, or something. There had to be something that they could do. A thoughtless but seemingly cruel doctor told me that there was no one available to do a scan. 'Anyway, we could find a heartbeat now and the foetus could be dead by morning.' Her words have never left me.

It was the next morning before we found out our baby's fate. I will never forget hearing the sonographer confirm that there was no heartbeat. I will never forget moving into the doctor's room to discuss whether I wanted an ERPC (evacuation of retained products of conception, which is basically the surgical removal of the foetal remains and pregnancy-related tissue) or to wait for 'nature to take its course'. I will never forget that surreal feeling leaving the hospital and going home to my toddler daughter, looking at her knowing the sibling we thought she would have was not to be. I will never forget the emptiness I felt the next day when I woke from the anaesthetic after the 'procedure' and I remembered my baby was gone.

Future pregnancies were overshadowed by my real fear and knowing that something could go wrong, and in between the births of other children, it did indeed go wrong three further times. Each time, my heart broke and ached for the baby that I hadn't managed to carry safely.

People often don't know what to say to you at the time and even well-intended comments and remarks can really hurt. Silence hurts just as much. I just wanted to have someone to talk to and recognise that I should have had that baby – that I was grieving for my baby.

That's one of the difficult things about miscarriage – everyone deals with it differently and it can be hard for the person looking in to know what to do and for the person going through it to know if their reaction is 'appropriate'. The truth is there is no right or wrong way to feel. There is only the way that you do feel.

The emotional recovery from miscarriage is often much more difficult than the physical one. Personally, I found talking helped. I found online parenting forums helped, where I could speak with other mums who had been through the same thing. I found having something tangible to touch and to remember my babies by also helped.

It's essential to be kind to yourself over the following weeks and months. As with everything, life moves on, but you're still coping with what has happened and the upset can catch up with you at the most unexpected times. Dates can mean a lot and how you mark them is a very personal thing. Others may forget or just not want to mention it, for fear of upsetting you.

It's important to remember you did nothing wrong. It wasn't your fault. Miscarriages can happen for many different reasons, most of which you cannot prevent. The majority of people who have a miscarriage (or miscarriages even) go on to have healthy babies in the future. Knowing when to try again is also a very personal decision. Some doctors suggest waiting until you've had at least one period, for ease of dating a future pregnancy. Some women want to try again immediately. Others want time to process their grief or reconsider their plans. The best time to try again is when you feel ready.

Four different angels hang on our Christmas tree every year, alongside individual decorations belonging to my seven children. They are my tangible memory and recognition of my four babies who started their journey but never completed it. I was very lucky; my beautiful rainbow babies came but the storm that preceded their arrival also shaped the person I became. Such are the mouldings of motherhood and its emotional and sometimes precarious journey.

2

Baby's First Year

Nothing can quite prepare you for the rush of emotions and abundance of feelings you will experience when baby is first born. Excitement, love, relief, a wondering of 'what the hell just happened', exhaustion and ecstasy can all flood through you at the same time. It's a pretty good reflection of the life that follows.

Baby grows at the fastest rate of their life during the early weeks and moves from a totally helpless newborn to developing a little personality of their own that will have you both smitten and wrapped around their tiny little finger in what seems like the blink of an eye. One thing not to underestimate, however, is the workload that this tiny person brings. Coupled with a newfound preoccupation with bodily fluids and the virtual obliteration of your 'ick' factor, you may find that all is changed, changed utterly, but that's not necessarily a bad thing.

While you'll learn exactly why sleep deprivation is used as a form of torture and grow to understand why so many mums consider taking a shower as an accomplishment, you'll also surprise yourself with the many things that you can achieve once you get into the swing of things. In addition, you'll appreciate very quickly why 'eat, poop, sleep, repeat' could be considered the mantra of every newborn baby.

The First Six Weeks

The first six weeks are often hailed as an exhausting period but I think the reality is that it's more of a learning period. Mum and dad are learning how to be parents, for the first time possibly, or at the very least how to be parents to this tiny new individual. Mum is recovering from childbirth. Hormone levels are dropping. There's a new dynamic at home and there are no midwives on hand to help and guide you.

This tiny little person appears so helpless, unable even to support their own head, and the initial prospect of their care can feel overwhelming. Newborn babies' needs are pretty simple though: love, warmth, food and security – and a good rugby hold for bathtime helps.

The Umbilical Stump

When baby comes home from hospital, chances are the umbilical stump will still be attached. It's very important to keep this clean and to not tug at it. Cool boiled water and cotton wool are ideal for cleaning the area. The stump generally falls off after a few days and often you'll find it in your baby's nappy during a change. If, in the interim, you notice the stump becoming smelly or oozing, always check with a medical professional to rule out the risk of infection.

Bathtime

Those first few baths are always a slightly nerve-wracking experience and learning how to ensure things run smoothly is a skill to be acquired in the early weeks. Lots of babies love bathtime, mine included, but plenty more are equally unsure.

In the early weeks, it can help to place a baby bath on a secure table and bathe baby there. This minimises the amount of bending necessary, which is particularly important for protecting your still vulnerable back, or a C-section wound if you have one. Always test the bathwater with your elbow and not your hand.

Newborns can be very slippery, so it might feel easier to wash their hair over the bath before placing them in it. The best way that I found to do this was to strip baby and wrap them in a towel to keep baby warm. Holding baby almost like a rugby ball, with baby's body tucked under my dominant arm, I could support their head with my hand. It meant I had a secure grip and baby felt secure too, so was quite happy to let me get on with washing their hair (or head as it were in my bald babies' cases) over the bath.

Once baby's hair is washed, the towel can be removed and baby is ready to go straight into the bath. You now have two free hands to keep close by your wriggly human eel.

Noisy Nights

Nighttime feeds are the not the only thing likely to keep you awake. Newborn babies make all sorts of weird and wonderful sounds, particularly in the early days. As long as the noises don't sound as if baby is having difficulty breathing, such as constant grunting, they are nothing to worry about and are often caused by baby having narrow nasal passages and mucus.

If the noise doesn't keep you awake, the silence will no doubt give you cause for concern, as you strain to hear your baby's near-soundless breathing. Chances are you'll wake baby at least once from their peaceful slumber through gentle prodding only to receive loud and vocal confirmation that all is well. It's an unavoidable rite of passage.

Baby Skin

The television ads may display images of babies with beautiful soft, clear skin but many babies are prone to dry and cracked skin in the first days and weeks after birth, particularly around their wrists and ankles. Moisturisers and warm (not hot) baths can help with the issue of dry skin.

Acne is another skin condition you might not expect but it turns out that acne is not just reserved for teenagers. Baby acne is very common as delicate skin adjusts to life outside the womb. Generally, baby acne appears on baby's cheeks. Keeping the affected area clean and dry can help as drool can agitate it (as can some fabrics). The acne usually clears up of its own accord and without any medical treatment.

Milia, or milk spots, are often visible at or appear shortly after birth. Unlike baby acne, there is no swelling or redness. Milia are small white bumps that generally disappear within a couple of weeks and cause no agitation to baby.

Baby typically has a check-up at six weeks old, which is the perfect opportunity to address any non-urgent concerns you may have. The first six weeks are usually the building blocks for the weeks and months ahead. Towards the end of this time, your hard work will hopefully be rewarded with the most precious of all first smile from your mini-me.

While the umbilical stump will fall off, the noises will die down and baby will learn to support their own head, the other stuff involved with babyhood continues beyond the first few weeks. As time passes, new challenges emerge but so do new rewards as you find yourself getting excited about the sort of things you never thought possible.

BREASTFEEDING

Breast is best, we've heard it said,
There's nothing can compare,
As long as practiced discreetly of course,
So people, they won't stare,
'Cos you might put them off their food,
If boobies they did see,
While trying to have a wrap or roll,
With their coffee or their tea,
And even if your baby cries,
With hunger for a feed,
Find somewhere out of people's gaze,
A toilet, if you need,
After all the comfort of mum and babe,
Is very important too,
And baby will still enjoy their lunch
Surrounded by wee and poo,
Exhibitionist mums, please be aware,

And think of others' feelings,
Don't whip 'em out for all to see,
Directing gazes to the ceilings,
'Cos boobs are fine for porn and mags,
For ads and TV maybe,
The only time they cause offence,
Is when you're feeding baby!

Every day it seems there is a celebrity somewhere sharing a 'brelfie' (breastfeeding selfie) on some form of social media, promoting breastfeeding's naturalness and positivity. In spite of this, in the land of mere mortals breastfeeding rates remain low and a significant number of misconceptions still surround this very natural process.

I was very fortunate in that breastfeeding worked well for me and was my saviour in many regards in terms of convenience as my numbers grew. It is, however, a new skill that mum and baby need to learn and perfect together, and like most new skills it can take a little time to master. Unfortunately, early difficulties and lack of support can mean women often decide not to continue with breastfeeding before they have a real chance to experience its many advantages.

While breastfeeding may not be for everyone, there are a few things that I found helped me on my breastfeeding journey and made it a very special and enjoyable part of motherhood.

Be Realistic About Your Expectations

This is probably one of the most important things about breastfeeding. A breastfed baby needs very frequent feeding, particularly in the early days and whenever a growth spurt occurs. This is necessary both in terms of satisfying baby's appetite and in helping your body to adjust the amount of milk it needs to make. A baby may last two hours between a feed or just twenty minutes. This doesn't mean, as many women misinterpret, that you are not producing enough milk. Cluster feeding is very normal, especially in the evening time when baby goes from one feed to another to another. The key is feeding on demand, demand, demand, however often that may be.

As baby gets older, a natural spread will occur between feeds and baby will become much more efficient at feeding too. This is when the real time-saving benefit sets in for you. With no bottles to sterilise and prepare, no milk to heat to the correct temperature and no fear of waste if baby only wants to graze, you can very much adopt the motto 'have boobs, will travel'. This has saved me on so many school runs and activity collections. Baby could have a quick five-minute feed beforehand and a top-up when we arrived at our destination. No time was ever lost – it was just latch on and go!

Slow Down, Sit Down and Feed

In the modern world, there can be a rush to get back to normal. A young baby throws most established routines out the window for a period and there's really nothing else to do but go with the flow. When it's time to feed – even if that's just half an hour after the last one – sit down, relax and take it as an enforced break. Fretting about all that has to be done won't change anything and housework can wait. This time won't last forever. Stopping and embracing the necessary feeding breaks not only gives you valuable bonding time with baby, but makes sure that you as a mum, who is still a person too, gets to rest and recover from the demands of new parenthood.

Remind Yourself of the Upside

In a sleep-deprived haze, it's easy to feel overwhelmed by the constant demands of looking after a young baby. With breastfeeding, most of the feeding falls to mum, unless you express milk of course, and that can add to a sense of frustration. It's important to remind yourself of the advantages every now and then, rather than just focusing on the restrictions, which is very easy to do when you're tired and frustrated.

There is huge convenience with breastfeeding, no need to sterilise bottles and no need to prepare feeds before leaving the house, including spares – just in case. Breastfeeding burns calories and helps you to regain your figure after childbirth.

Breastfeeding also offers significant health benefits to both you and baby. The antibodies in breastmilk help baby to fight off viruses and bacteria. Being breastfed can reduce the incidences of ear infections, respiratory illnesses, urinary tract infections, gastrointestinal infections and bouts of diarrhoea, and reduces the risk of baby developing allergies. It can also offer protection against Type 1 and Type 2 diabetes, lymphoma, leukaemia, Hodgkin's disease and SIDS (Sudden Infant Death Syndrome). For mum, the health benefits include a lower risk of breast and ovarian cancer, reduced risk of heart disease, a lower risk of osteoporosis and a lower risk of developing Type 2 diabetes in the years after delivery. So remind yourself on a tough day, you're not just a milking machine. In addition to providing nutrition, comfort and a wonderful bonding experience, breastfeeding is protecting the health of both you and baby for now and years to come.

Feeding in Public

There is a time and place for breastfeeding. That time is whenever baby is hungry, and the place is wherever you want and need to be.

Although a breastfeeding mother is entitled by law to feed her baby wherever she wants, some women feel a little more reluctant and nervous. Being comfortable feeding in public is a big advantage as it means you're less likely to feel the cabin fever of being trapped at home. If you are a little wary, taking a friend or family member along with you the first time can really help. As well as providing moral support, they can also be a person to chat with over a coffee and hopefully provide a welcome distraction.

Wearing a vest or camisole under your top can also help you to feel less exposed when feeding and it has the added bonus of turning all of your shirts and tops into breastfeeding wear.

Pain

Breastfeeding shouldn't hurt. In the early days while you and baby are perfecting the latch it is possible that your nipples can become sore and cracked. Lanolin cream is a big help here and can be applied directly before a feed. However, if pain is ongoing, ask your midwife, lactation consultant or public health nurse for advice and guidance. Also, don't underestimate the invaluable support and advice a breastfeeding friend or relative might be able to offer.

Breastfeeding Support

While only mum can breastfeed, other members of the family and friends can help in a variety of ways. Support is really important, particularly in the early days and weeks as the new skill is learned and the adjustment to the new family dynamic takes place. Partners can help through encouragement and through practical assistance such as getting a glass of water for mum (because breastfeeding can make you feel really thirsty), helping more around the house and with other children, and by helping with baby in the many other aspects of care that are required. Breastfeeding does not mean dad needs to feel left out. There are so many other ways dad can bond and spend time with baby – such as bathing, nappy changing and cuddles – which also give mum an opportunity to rest and recuperate.

Sometimes when a mum is struggling, or because it's not a well-meaning person's norm, she can be subjected to comments such as 'you've given him/her the best start – why not move to formula now?' Even though these sorts of comments are often meant in a supportive manner, they can make you feel undermined, particularly if you have not expressed a desire to stop breastfeeding. If the comments are likely to recur it's worth mentioning to the person that you would prefer to focus on continuing and all support would be much appreciated.

There are many supports available to mums (and dads even), such as breastfeeding preparation classes ahead of baby's birth, which give the opportunity to discuss any concerns and allow the lactation consultant the opportunity to flag any potential difficulties such as flat or inverted nipples, while discussing how any potential issues might be overcome. Classes also provide dads with the opportunity to learn how they can support their partners on their breastfeeding journeys and are a great way of helping dads to get involved too.

Breastfeeding support groups are a wonderful way to meet other mums whose babies are at a similar stage of life and provide a nice comfortable environment to ask questions. Many local health centres also host their own breastfeeding groups and frequently the public health nurse is on hand to weigh baby too. Online forums and Facebook support groups can also provide practical support and information, while private lactation consultants are available for assistance, guidance and support.

Friends and relatives who have breastfed or are breastfeeding can be an untapped wealth of information. Don't be afraid to ask advice. Sometimes it might not be forthcoming without request, for fear of overstepping the mark.

Every breastfeed you give your baby has benefits for both of you so give yourself a pat on the back and credit yourself for every single one that you achieve. Don't get too caught up in targets. Take it one day at a time and you may well surprise yourself by managing to breastfeed longer than you thought possible in those early, sometimes trickier, days.

SLEEP

No doubt you'll have heard plenty of times over the course of your pregnancy, and even after your little one's arrival, that sleep would become a distant memory. Having been blessed with seven non-sleepers I'm afraid I can't offer any words of comfort here, except to say that it doesn't last forever. Try not to be disheartened if everyone else seems to have babies who sleep idyllically. My experience has been that parents aren't always completely honest about their babies sleeping (or crying habits for that matter).

The Early Days and Weeks

The heat of the hospital and the efforts of being born mean new babies are often very sleepy in the first couple of days and can lull us poor unsuspecting parents into a false sense of security. When we arrive home to more normal and recommended temperatures it can be a shock to the system to find that baby is no longer as keen on the virtues of slumber.

Newborns typically sleep for sixteen to seventeen hours a day. Most new babies, however, generally don't sleep for more than two to four hours at a time, regardless of whether it's day or night. The constant disturbance to our own sleep can make it feel as though baby sleeps much less than they really do.

As newborn babies' stomachs are very small, they can only hold very tiny amounts of milk. Waking frequently for feeds is both natural and essential. As the weeks pass, baby becomes capable of sleeping for a slightly longer stretch, but just because they're capable doesn't make them willing. Crueller still is the fact that when baby does manage to string a couple of hours sleep together it's rarely at a time that you can take advantage. We spent many a night driving around at 3 a.m. in a desperate effort to get our daughter to sleep. As soon as the car moved she was out for the count, but she never made the transition to her waiting cot smoothly. Her dad and I spent those first few months wandering around in a sleep-deprived stupor. My hubby even managed to travel all the way home from work on the bus one day, miss his stop and make it halfway back to work again before he woke up.

By baby number two, I learned all about the power of the cat nap. This time I realised and fully appreciated the validity of the mantra 'this too shall pass'; therefore I prioritised sleep over loading the dishwasher when my sleep-resistant son finally had forty winks.

As the Months Pass

There is really no hard and fast rule as to when babies will finally sleep through the night. The important thing to remember is that all babies are different. Some settle into beautiful sleep patterns at a few months old while others hit their first birthday still unconvinced of the merits of sleep. Mine, unfortunately, fell into the latter category and eventually needed some coaxing to sleep through the night. A year-and-a-half of sleep deprivation was generally enough to motivate me to tackle the issue, in desperate pursuit of some much needed zzzz's.

There are things that can be done to greatly assist improving baby's sleep and a few things to avoid:

- Keep a consistent routine: bath, feed, story/song and bed. The consistency indicates to baby that it's bedtime and they know what to expect. The bath helps to relax baby and tire baby out. If possible, try to keep bedtime to a similar time each night.
- Don't be tempted to skip daytime naps. Not only will you have a very cranky baby to deal with during the day but an overtired baby will be even more difficult to settle at night and most likely will wake more frequently.
- Watch out for tiredness cues such as yawning, rubbing eyes and crying, and act on them as soon as possible to avoid overtiredness.
- Easier said than done, but try to avoid the habit of an older baby/ toddler falling asleep on a feed. Where possible put your little one down for a nap while sleepy, but not quite asleep. This means that if they wake a short time later, they should find it easier to settle themselves again rather than wondering where mum, who was there when they drifted off, has suddenly disappeared to.

Where to Sleep

Best-laid plans can face a dramatic overhaul when the prospect of little or no sleep exists. While some parents adamantly declare that their child will always sleep in their own cot, others prefer to co-sleep, sharing their bed and keeping baby close by.

I am, and always have been, a fan of whatever gets you the most sleep, while following safety rules of course. My babies always began their night's slumber in the comfort of their Moses basket or cot but, without fail, at some stage during the night each joined us in our seemingly much more comfortable bed. Any attempts to relocate them back to their beautifully dressed and carefully chosen character-themed beds were met with middle-of-the-night wails and protests.

Sleep deprivation has a cumulative effect. As the days go by, it catches up on you. By the end of the first week, you'll forget what you went upstairs for. Two weeks in and you've given up trying to remember your other children's names, the alarm code, or the day of the week. Two months on and you may, as I did, find yourself drawing a blank when the optician's assistant asks your name and attempt to justify your delay in responding with a mumbled excuse that the baby doesn't rate sleep, while she looks at you incredulously, obviously regarding you as some sort of mad woman.

And so I found myself on each occasion as an unintended co-sleeper, for part of the night anyway. It was easier for breastfeeding certainly. Baby drifted back to sleep quite quickly and we avoided the midnight meltdowns with no need to transfer. The end result was that I got a lot more sleep (in the early months at least).

Keeping Baby Safe

Keeping baby safe is a priority, whatever sleeping arrangement you choose. The recommendations are that baby sleeps in their own bed with baby's feet at the foot of the cot. Baby should always be placed on their back and should not use a pillow if under the age of one year.

It's important not to let baby overheat so the number of blankets should be adjusted according to the temperature. The room temperature should be ideally between 16 and 20 degrees Celsius. Blankets should be tucked under baby's arms (cellular blankets are ideal as they allow air to circulate), though some people prefer to use a baby sleeping bag.

To reduce the risk of Sudden Infant Death Syndrome (SIDS), baby should sleep in the same room as their parents until at least the age of six months (though a recent study has suggested twelve months as preferable). Babies have been shown to imitate their mothers' breathing pattern when they share a room.

Never share a bed with your baby if you have been drinking or smoking or are especially tired. If baby does share your bed, do not cover them with your duvet. Use baby's own blankets and never use a pillow.

Helping Things Along

My children didn't fall into wonderful sleeping habits unaided. It took some encouragement, but eighteen months of broken sleep that got progressively worse rather than better was enough to spur us on. Never one for allowing my children to cry themselves to sleep, we took a different approach, which has thankfully worked well on each occasion.

The first part of the equation involved helping baby to fall asleep in the cot and not in my arms while still attached to my boob. Some of my children used soothers, but most didn't. This method, however, worked either way. Baby generally was unimpressed at being placed in the cot awake so my husband stayed right beside them for the first couple of days, picking baby up if they became distressed and constantly reassuring the baby that he was there. The reason that it was my husband who settled the baby, in the early stage at least, was that I, or more accurately my boobs, was associated with feeding at bedtime and it was less stressful for both of us.

As the days passed my husband moved slightly further away from the cot and closer to the door, eventually moving outside it. Baby knew what to expect and there were no longer bedtime protests. We never left baby to cry, always reassuring baby that we were there.

After a few days, it became possible for me to put baby to bed as the initial feed-to-sleep association was broken. Falling asleep on their own saw the beginning of a longer period of sleep, but the middle of the night waking still had to be tackled.

An inevitable game of musical beds was necessary when that time came. When the baby woke during the night for the first time, I fed them. At this stage baby was eighteen months old, so definitely not nutritionally in need of a nighttime feed but I was very aware of how much comfort it offered to my respective babies, which is why I didn't want to withdraw it suddenly.

I brought the baby into our bed, fed baby and once they had drifted back to sleep I left my bed and a sleeping baby beside my husband. When baby woke, he comforted and soothed baby. Because

I wasn't there, it was easier for my husband to comfort the baby as my absence meant I wasn't in effect denying baby anything.

As with everything, the first couple of nights were the most difficult. Baby woke frequently, as was their norm, but because I didn't feed baby during the night (except at that first waking), baby stopped waking altogether. In our case, one thing led to another and night-weaning, consequentially, meant that our little one decided that it wasn't worth getting up if nothing was on offer.

The reality of a full night's sleep was great for everyone. Besides having more energy ourselves, our babies were in better form and more predictability followed in terms of our daytime structure. Of course some nights babies wake up for no particular reason, or because they're teething, unsettled or ill. Personally, I have never minded our children coming into our bed as long as they slept – after all, it's rare enough to hear of a sixteen-year-old who still does it.

Poo

The world of poo will never be a source of such fascination for you as it will be when baby arrives. And never again will it be considered a socially acceptable conversation piece – amongst certain quarters only of course.

You will learn much on your journey through the various colours and textures of baby poo – from the first days' black, sticky, tar-like produce, to the mustard, supposedly 'sweet-smelling' stuff, to the days after solids have been introduced and you can visibly confirm that baby did in fact eat his corn. At some stage you will experience a poo-nami* firsthand and realise that while the yellow stuff generally indicates that baby's health is well, it is a nightmare to get out of babygros and jeans.

---

* Poo-nami: an incredibly explosive nappy, which results in most of the pooey contents going up the baby's back, soaking through every stich of their clothes and most likely writing off yours too. Sod's law dictates that it occurs most frequently when you are out somewhere and/or wearing pale clothes.

TIME-KEEPING

If you're the sort of person who thinks baby will just fit into your routine – well good luck with that one. Babies are predictably unpredictable and just as you plan to leave the house you can be completely certain that the aforementioned poo-nami will occur, an uncontrollable hunger will hit, or an expertly directed burp and follow-through will redesign your, up until then, perfectly clean clothes. Don't worry though because anyone who has ever had a baby knows that the most important word in 'ETA' is estimated.

To minimise your own stress, always factor in extra time, or if your other half happens to be the one who underestimates the time involved in getting out of the house with baby (which *may* be the case in this house), just tell them that you're due to be there an hour earlier than you actually are.

MILESTONES

Right from birth we all eagerly await that first milestone baby is supposed to meet, which is somewhere around the six-week mark – the first smile. While some will do it right on cue, some will meet the milestone earlier and others will leave their adoring parents waiting that bit longer.

The first year is filled with anticipation of baby's many and various milestones. From sitting and crawling (or bum-shuffling) to standing and walking. From the first pearly white tooth appearing to the much-anticipated first word. But while there are general guidelines about when these milestones can be expected, they are largely just that – guidelines.

Even within the same family there can be a variation of several months between siblings meeting milestones without it being an indication of any problems. We've had some twelve-month walkers here and some who needed active encouragement at eighteen months. We've had one baby born with a tooth and two who were still toothless on their first birthdays, and we've had some who crawled early and some who were very efficient bum-shufflers who bypassed crawling completely.

Check-ups with your public health nurse are an excellent opportunity to highlight any concerns you may have. In addition to checking baby's weight, length and head circumference, the nurse will speak to you about baby's progress in a number of areas and suggest some aids for minor issues.

Try not to be fazed by other mums highlighting their babies' successes and achievements at a younger age. Aside from the fact that every baby is different, sometimes mums get caught up in the inherent pride and love they feel for their little ones and exaggeration can be the order of the day. Also, it's worth bearing in mind that while most mums are keen supporters of each other, there are, as in every walk of life, always the competitive few who can inadvertently add to your worries.

However, if you are genuinely concerned, speak with your public health nurse or general practitioner: they are the experts in this field and the people best placed to guide you.

CRYING

There are no hard and fast rules here and crying really does vary from baby to baby. Some babies cry very little and seem settled straight from birth. Others arrive into the world announcing their arrival loudly and continue in the same fashion to remind everyone that they are still here. Some babies completely wrong-foot us by starting off quiet and calm, only to become more vocal down the line.

Baby's new world is a million miles away from the safe and familiar environment of the womb. Sounds are different, textures and smells are different, and most of all they're no longer physically attached to their mother. It's no wonder that some babies become a little fretful and are in need of being held. In your arms, they can hear your heartbeat and know your smell. They can feel safe and secure again and are less confused by their new surroundings.

Seven children on and I still cannot bear to hear a baby cry. My solution: I pick them up immediately. I'm a great believer in responding to baby's needs as soon as possible – even if that need is just a cuddle. I don't believe that babies cry for no reason and I think wanting to be with mum or dad is as good a reason as any.

We've had a combination of every type of baby mentioned in the first paragraph and there is no denying that prolonged crying is very difficult to manage. With our first baby, colic was the diagnosed cause for her incessant tears and while the three-month period until it passed was extremely difficult for her and us, there was a certain relief in knowing that there was a cause. It also enabled us to try out some of the tactics suggested to alleviate the symptoms.

Baby number two was born smiling and stayed smiling his entire babyhood. I was advised by others to leave him in his baby rocker and not to carry him too often or else I would create bad habits. I ignored that advice. He was a happy little dude and I didn't want him to pay the price of a lack of cuddles for that reason. Needless to say, it was just his personality and the fortunate circumstance that he didn't have colic. All the cuddles in the world didn't stop him from being the most placid, relaxed baby of them all – even when he was put back down.

It's difficult to know how much crying to expect the first time around but there are a few things to check as the potential cause:

- Is baby hungry?
- Does baby need a change of nappy?
- Is baby warm/cool enough?
- Are baby's clothes comfortable and not causing irritation?
- Is baby in need of being held?
- Is baby tired?
- Does baby have wind?
- Is baby in pain or is something hurting baby?

If none of these things seem to be the cause of baby's upset and prolonged crying continues then it's time to consider speaking to your GP or PHN, who may be able to get to the bottom of baby's crying and help you to find a solution. If you feel baby may be ill, trust your instincts and don't delay in taking baby to the doctor.

As the months pass, babies generally cry less as they find new ways of communicating and interacting with those around them. Cooing and babbling become part of their language and as the ability to handle and manoeuvre objects improves they find ways of communicating that are much more pleasant to the ears.

Weaning

Around the age of six months, baby will be ready to move on from a milk-only diet. Often parents can feel the pressure to start baby on solids before baby is ready as a result of well-intended but ill-informed advice that baby is obviously hungry and that giving them solids will help them to sleep through the night. (Can I at this stage refer you back to that section on my sleep-resisting babies?) Before the age of six months, baby's digestive system is not mature enough for solid foods. So, if baby seems hungry, increasing the amount of milk feeds is the correct route to take.

Taking the first step and giving baby his first taste of 'proper' food can be a nerve-wrecking experience. The texture, as well as the taste, is new and even the most pureed and liquidised concoctions can still result in a gagging reaction.

Choose a time when baby is not too hungry to begin the weaning process. Babies will only eat very tiny amounts at the beginning. With my older children, the first food I offered to them was baby rice. They weren't particularly keen, so with the younger children I offered pureed fruits as a first food. I offered one food at a time so that, in addition to helping them to get used to the taste, I could observe their reaction and ensure that they didn't have any allergies.

Weaning is quite a slow process and for many days, weeks even, baby may well be content with just one meal a day. I allowed baby's appetite to dictate the amount and frequency of their solid feeds. I often gave baby a plastic bowl and spoon to hold at the same time I fed them. Sometimes I put a tiny bit of food in the bowl and baby helped themselves to the contents while I offered spoon feeds. It's messy but it worked. What is important to remember is that baby still needs most of their nutrition from their milk at this stage.

While most of the time baby ate homemade food, I sometimes used baby dinners purchased in the shop during the weaning process. While it was easy to freeze food that I had made at home and defrost as required, I liked the added benefit and convenience of knowing that baby would eat a jar if I was caught short somewhere and it was necessary. I also found that the baby jars helped when there was a transition to the next stage of food consistency. They always seemed to get it spot on.

As with everything else, different children are more receptive to the weaning process than others. Establishing good habits early is important, so don't be put off by a baby's refusal to try a food one day. Just offer the same food to them again in the days that follow.

There are some foods that should be avoided and are unsuitable for babies:

- Raw or partially cooked eggs
- Honey
- Cow's milk is an unsuitable replacement for breastmilk or formula but can be used to prepare baby's food once baby is six months or older.
- Salt or sugar should never be added to baby's food.
- Low-fat foods should be avoided.

As baby's digestive system adjusts to its new food offerings, there can sometimes be a difficulty with constipation. Making sure baby is offered plenty of fluids can help here, ideally in the form of water and their usual milk.

Another thing to be aware of is that those alleged sweet-smelling nappies of purely breastfed days are about to become a thing of the past. Once solids have commenced no one will be in any doubt that baby has pooed.

***

Things move and change very quickly in the first twelve months as baby and parents get to know each other. While it's a year full of hard work, tiredness and more poo than you can imagine, it's also a year full of cuddles, love and fabulous firsts.

By the end of it you'll have some idea of the personality of the little person you're raising and you'll know whether you have a relaxed little one who will take everything in their stride or a mischievous little rascal who plans to keep you on your toes. Either way the fun, challenges and non-stop learning continues.

3

Being Mum – Challenging Times

The birth of a first baby also brings the birth of a first-time parent, while the birth of subsequent children brings a whole new dynamic to the family. Motherhood is often played out on social media as an idyllic time, full of picture-perfect moments, some with filter, some without – largely depending on the level of tears, tantrums and breakdowns involved ahead of that perfect snap.

These social media moments rarely reflect the true reality of the sometimes monotonous days and the never-ending workload. Pictures of snot-bubble-blowing babies against the backdrop of a house that looks like it has been turned over by burglars, comparatively, rarely make their way onto the various social media platforms.

Motherhood isn't just about baby; it's also about a new you, in a role that you can't completely prepare for. Practical preparations don't allow for feelings, and the intensity of feelings that you'll have for this little person – in spite of the large quantities of snot and poo they can produce, in spite of the fact that it's usually a one-way conversation, and in spite of the fact that they inflict tortuous levels of sleep deprivation upon you – can be more than a little overwhelming.

While you may have sworn prior to baby's arrival that you would continue certain aspects of your life in a similar fashion to before, the realities of grappling with the demands that go hand-in-hand with having a young child can lead you to feeling cut off from the world around you and a very different person to the one you used to know.

But you're not different, you're still you – you just have a different perspective on things. Looking after yourself is just as important as looking after baby. The saying 'happy mum equals happy baby' isn't just a phrase that's loosely thrown around; it's a true and valid statement.

Parenthood is a learning curve for everyone. It doesn't just teach you about children, what to expect and how to take care of them. Parenthood teaches you about yourself, your strengths and vulnerabilities, and brings new challenges and lessons to the table.

While discovering the new you and trying to find your feet in the world of parenting, it's important to remember that you are not alone. The rewards of parenthood are well-documented and celebrated, but the challenges of early parenthood, in particular, are faced by us all. Therefore, knowing what to expect, acknowledging that many mums feel the same, and understanding how to help yourself muddle through the many adjustments can play a big part in the reconciliation between the old and new you.

A LONELY TIME

They say it takes a village to rear a child but these days the villagers all seem to be busy, off doing their own thing. The first days after baby's birth are often filled with excited visitors, as newly appointed grandparents, aunts and uncles come to dote on the newest member of the family, while friends stop by with gifts and words of admiration. Excitement is at an all-time high. Baby (and hopefully you too), is the focal point of everyone's good wishes, concerns and delight. But when those initial days pass, the visitors slow down and a new and unfamiliar normality takes hold, feelings of loneliness and isolation can creep in.

Taking care of babies and young children can be all-consuming. In addition to subjecting their parents to the progressive and cumulative effects of broken sleep, planning a trip outdoors with a baby or young child generally requires military-style planning and often the packing of half the house's contents.

Great plans can be made to get out and purchase that badly needed pint of milk but following an hour spent dressing and redressing yourself and baby, after a poo explosion leaked through baby's nappy, writing off their first-time-worn babygro, and leaving a giant yellow/green stain on your clean jeans in the process, the efforts involved can sometimes appear to outweigh any benefit. Add to the equation the fact that you now have approximately fifteen minutes to load up the buggy and get to and from the shops before baby lets everyone know with their powerful lungs and impressive pitch that it's feeding time once again, and your convictions that you should just stay put seem even more justified.

It's easy to fall into bad habits and if nobody calls to see you either, you can find the whole day passes without any adult interaction. Unlike the days of yesteryear, there is a less collaborative approach in society to parenting, as women are not necessarily giving birth at the same time as their peers. With more women working outside the home, friends and neighbours are not necessarily around during the day. The sense of community is different to our own parents' time and many mums live a distance from their families.

It's not easy to reach out and admit you're feeling lonely. It seems a contradiction in terms to say you're lonely when getting a moment to yourself is one of the biggest challenges of motherhood, but we all need adult company and stimulation. We're social creatures by nature. The big shock to the system can be the realisation that if you want company you may well have to ask for it or get out there and find it.

OVERCOMING LONELINESS AND ISOLATION

Ask for Visitors and Help

People don't necessarily mean to abandon you and leave you to your own devices when baby comes along, but in the confusion about the busyness of motherhood, friends and family can think that they are giving you space and time to get to know your baby and to get on with your busy life. Those who have never had children may not even be aware of the isolation you feel – so tell them. Tell them that you'd love if they popped in for a cuppa and a chat. Tell them that you'd love if, instead of meeting you somewhere, they could come to your house to help you to get organised, so that you could go to your planned destination together.

My tardiness when I had a new baby was a sore point for me. I felt frustrated when people teased me for running late, even though it was only ever in jest. I felt they couldn't appreciate the frustration and efforts involved in loading the car and getting out. Even after having several children, my latest arrival could always hold me to ransom with a stinker of a nappy just as I was about to leave the house, or the deposit of a regurgitated feed in my just brushed hair – brushed you'll note, not washed, because if I was to have a morning shower then I'd never manage to get out of the house. The days a friend came to the house and held and soothed my baby while I cleaned my teeth, put on my shoes and grabbed my coat, ready to face civilisation, or at least the inhabitants of the local park, made my life so much easier.

Mum Friends

I was twenty-four when I was pregnant with my first child. None of my friends at the time were even on the same wavelength as me. I had no idea what lay in store and it certainly wasn't on their radar yet. They came to visit me in hospital when my daughter was born; one even mentioned how big my tummy still was, which I mention not because I'm still sensitive about it (promise) but to illustrate how clueless she, and indeed I, was about the whole 'having a baby' business.

When I returned home, my friends called sporadically and over the phone we chatted about nights out, what was going on in work and what their weekend plans were. We no longer seemed to be on the same planet. Our priorities had changed, as had our expectations and experiences of life. I realised that I was missing the company of people with whom I had something in common. Whether we were the same age or not was irrelevant. What mattered was that we were at the same stage of life – I needed mum friends.

Trying to make friends as an adult is obviously very different to trying to make friends as a child. Walking up to a stranger in the playground and asking them if they want to hang out, just because they have a buggy too, is likely to have them running in the opposite direction and possibly reporting your suspicious and strange behaviour on a parenting forum.

Thankfully there are some groups out there where chatting with people you don't know over a nice cuppa is not only welcomed but is actively encouraged. Mother and baby/toddler groups and breastfeeding support groups are often held in local health centres, community centres or parish halls. Your public health nurse will usually have details of meetings or a quick Google will throw out locations and times. These groups are an invaluable resource for mums of babies and toddlers, providing not only a great opportunity to meet new friends but also an opportunity to discuss any concerns or questions you may have. The great thing about these groups is that they're made up of mums who are at a similar stage of life and are managing similar restrictions and dealing with similar challenges.

Mum friends are essential, as they are friends who can appreciate where you are in your life. They can appreciate why, at this present moment, a night on the tiles might not hold the same appeal, but that doesn't mean you've forgotten what it is like to have fun. They can understand how an unsettled baby can turn the best-laid plans on their head. They can also recognise how precious your limited free time is and why a mum's night out usually involves careful forward planning.

Online parenting forums can be another great way to meet mums, contrary to what we tell our children about the dangers of talking to strangers on the internet. They're a place to chat and talk online about parenting concerns, but many forums also have a meet-up board for mums to meet other local mums. I've made a few mum friends this way and it has always been lovely to put a face to the username. Just in case any of my children read this, rest assured I always met the mums in a public place and more often than not in a group situation.

Mother and Baby Activities

There are many activities geared towards mums and their babies which mean elements of our past pre-mum lives don't need to be entirely abandoned. What's more, the fact that it's a mum-and-baby session means you have no need to feel self-conscious if your baby has a vocal meltdown or breaks wind loudly in company.

Yoga, swimming lessons and even mother-and-baby cinema clubs have all become the rage in recent years, giving mums the opportunity to get some valuable exercise and catch up on the latest cinema releases. These are all also excellent ways to get out and meet other mothers. It may feel a huge task to get organised enough to attend these activities, and tiredness can certainly be a huge demotivating factor, but they're definitely worth the effort.

Baby massage classes are another popular choice with mums. Not only are they another opportunity to meet mothers but through the classes you can learn fantastic calming techniques for your baby, which may even lead to improved sleep – who doesn't want that?

Be the Hostess with the Mostest

If you know a few other mothers locally, inviting some around for a mid-morning cuppa can be an easy way to catch up. Don't stress with the preparation, a few biscuits or shop-bought scones with a pot of tea or coffee will do the trick. It's the conversation and outlet people will be coming for, not to judge your domestic goddess skills. If it works out, it may be something that can become a regular occurrence with different mums hosting on different occasions. Along with providing a regular social outlet, it means that no one solely feels the pressure of having to find somewhere to hide the visible clutter all the time.

Loneliness and isolation can be difficult aspects of motherhood to deal with, but they needn't last indefinitely. As baby grows, more predictability will follow and getting out and about, without quite as much planning or paraphernalia, will become a reality. The important thing in trying to overcome these lonely periods is to reach out and get out – and the rest will follow.

POSTNATAL DEPRESSION

The days after birth are an emotional rollercoaster. Not only are you coping with the exhaustive fallout of having given birth, but your hormones are dropping at a rapid level and your milk comes in for good measure. Up to 80 per cent of new mums are thought to experience some degree of the 'baby blues' as the after-effects of childbirth kick in. Tearfulness, sadness, anxiety and feelings of being overwhelmed are all very common symptoms of the baby blues, which thankfully for most women settle down somewhere between a few days and two weeks later. A smaller percentage of women, however, will go on to experience postnatal or postpartum depression. This is often mistaken for the baby blues at the beginning but the symptoms are more intense and they don't pass over.

Symptoms of Postnatal Depression

The symptoms of postnatal depression are quite broad and vary from one woman to another, but they include:

- Tearfulness
- Crying
- Anxiety
- Persistent sadness
- Reduced appetite
- Weight loss or weight gain
- Difficulty sleeping
- Difficulty concentrating
- Irritability
- Feelings of apathy
- Lack of interest in the baby
- Feeling overwhelmed
- Loss of pleasure in the things you used to enjoy

- Withdrawing from family and social circles
- Lacking in motivation
- Lacking in confidence
- Guilt
- Loss of libido
- Thoughts of harming yourself or baby

It's really important to remember that postnatal depression is indiscriminate; it can affect anyone. There are, however, some factors that can make a woman more vulnerable; these include:

- A history of postnatal depression
- A history of previous depression
- A traumatic pregnancy or childbirth experience
- A lack of support from partner, family or friends
- A stressful event such as the death of someone close, illness or job loss
- A baby with health worries or problems
- Financial worries

Postnatal depression typically occurs a few weeks after baby's birth, but sometimes it can appear more than six months later. In my case, however, it began almost immediately after the birth of my first child.

My Story

It has never really sat easy with me that I suffered with postnatal depression. It's not something that I'm particularly vocal about and until now I've never even written about it. It has happened following the births of six of my seven children and sometimes I wonder if that's why I'm so uneasy with it. How could it keep happening to me with all my experience?

I knew about the sleepless nights, I knew about the intensity of feelings and overwhelming sense of responsibility. I knew about the restrictions and I knew that I'd miss my bump, even if it had been the cause of a duck-like waddle for the three months preceding birth, and also made me forget what my toes looked like. I knew the demands that went hand-in-hand with having a new baby. I knew that it was a life-changing experience. I knew that the family dynamic would change. I knew how busy I'd be, but I also knew that each stage was a passing phase that wouldn't last forever. I knew that the initial mayhem would pass and a new, more comfortable and familiar mayhem would take its place. Yet, in spite of all this knowing and confidence in my convictions, the debilitating sadness returned so many times, casting its shadow over those precious early days, weeks and months.

It hit almost immediately after the birth of my first child. Following an extremely fast and furious delivery, our baby daughter arrived into the world, beautiful but shocked, and after I was given a very quick hold she was placed into an incubator as she was struggling to regulate her temperature. We were elated and I was in total self-awe at having grown this gorgeous little lady, and having survived childbirth if I'm honest about it. (What is it they say about self-praise being no praise?)

All feelings of exhaustion quickly passed as my daughter was returned to me and we were wheeled to the ward while I was still grinning like the proverbial Cheshire cat, the proudest mum ever – since the last mum to give birth of course. My husband stayed a short while, until we were settled in, and then headed home, delighted with himself. It was the middle of the night and I was alone with our baby girl, ready to take on my newfound responsibilities.

Few people seem to get a good night's sleep on a postnatal ward, though judging from the noisy snores coming from one of the beds opposite me it appears that there are always exceptions to that rule. When my daughter woke, I fed her but she didn't seem content. Minutes later she started to make funny noises, smacking her lips almost, and my novice-like gut instinct kicked in.

I called the midwife, who seemed initially bemused at my suggestion that something was wrong, but when she witnessed the continued noises she sent for the paediatrician. A few minutes later my baby was transferred to the Special Care Baby Unit (SCBU).

My daughter was having trouble regulating her blood sugar levels and spent the first two days of our time in hospital in the SCBU. It wasn't anything overly serious but I found the separation agonising. I felt like I wasn't doing my job properly – I wasn't protecting her. The sight of the cannula in her tiny hand left me distraught and tearful. I didn't sleep or even try to. I spent every moment I could with her, even during the night. My anxiety levels were climbing and kind suggestions made by the midwives that I should rest and they'd call me if there was an issue fell on deaf ears.

On the afternoon of the third day, while on the phone to my husband, updating him on our daughter's progress, a nurse arrived at the end of my bed with my baby in her arms. My shrieks of delight left ringing in my husband's ears for several days that followed, but I was so happy to have my baby girl back with me. She was there for me to touch, hold, love and care for as I wanted. Natural order was restored, but the tears kept coming.

The notes in my hospital chart appeared to sing my praises: 'Mum well and very independent with care' – the ultimate compliment for a first-timer. As we drove home the next day, with my precious bundle safely in her car seat beside me, I cried. I cried constantly as the days passed. I'd been warned about the baby blues and how they would coincide with my milk coming in, but these feelings of sadness were so intense and constant. If my husband decided to take our dog for a walk, I cried because I didn't want to be left alone. I didn't want to shower or bathe alone. I didn't want to do anything that involved me being alone, though I didn't know why.

My public health nurse at the time was one of a kind. She spotted my tearfulness the first day she called to see the baby. She suggested that I bring the baby for a weekly weigh-in and at those weigh-ins she always brought up how I felt. One week I didn't go and she appeared at the house. In a kind and unassuming manner, she suggested that it might be time for me to speak with a doctor. I didn't want to. I told her there was no point as I wouldn't take any medication anyway: 'I didn't want to get addicted to it.'

It's amazing how stubborn an uninformed person can be. I knew nothing about the different treatment options available, medical or otherwise, and yet I was adamant it wasn't for me. I was healthy, my baby was healthy. I felt I had no right to feel the way I felt. I needed to snap out of it.

Us mums can be incredibly hard on ourselves and I was no different. While I was pregnant there was never a problem with anyone suggesting that I take care of myself – after all it was in the best interests of my baby. I loved being pregnant. I loved that my baby was always with me and even the many pregnancy niggles were never enough to stop me feeling totally wonderstruck at being part of this whole amazing miracle. I felt almost too lucky to deserve it. When baby was born, however, in my eyes, I didn't deserve any special consideration. I was just Jen then, not Jen, mum-to-be. I wasn't special anymore. No baby depended on me. Nothing should be about me anymore; it should all be about baby.

Even as I write, I can see the irony. Of course my baby depended on me. Just because she was no longer in my womb didn't mean she didn't need me but depression clouded my view and judgement.

One day, after a particularly fraught morning, during which my daughter cried and cried as if echoing how I felt, I picked up the phone and rang my mother-in-law. I don't know how she understood me. I was inconsolable. 'The baby won't stop crying', I told her. 'I've tried everything.' 'I'm on my way', she said.

And so she arrived and the baby stopped crying. My mother-in-law kindly suggested that I take a bit of time out, maybe go to the hairdressers and have a bit of 'me' time. Sounds idyllic to most people but for me it was torture. In my head, it seemed crazy to decline. How could I explain to her that the suggestion of being apart from my baby filled me with anxiety and fear? I couldn't, so I didn't. I went down to the local shopping centre and waited for an acceptable amount of time to pass so I could go home. Instead of browsing in the shops or having my hair done, I hid in the toilets and cried and clock-watched.

I will always be grateful to the public health nurse who never gave up trying to coax me to see my GP. Even when I told her I was going to try some more natural methods to help me feel like myself again, she suggested that they sounded great, but reiterated that there was no harm in speaking with the doctor too. 'Happy mum equals happy baby' are the words that finally got me to the doctor's surgery. The suggestion that if I wasn't happy my darling daughter might not be either meant I had to do something – for her, not for me, because I wasn't important.

I was prescribed antidepressants and anti-anxiety medication. I hated how the anti-anxiety medication made me feel so I only took it once, but I continued with the antidepressants. As the weeks passed and without me really noticing when or why or how, I began to feel a little less sad. I began to stop lamenting that my daughter was no longer in my womb but instead appreciated that she was in my arms, still safe and still mine. I even began to enjoy leaving the house again. One outing to a neighbours' housewarming led me to meet an incredible woman who became a close friend and helped me put myself back together again. Piece by piece, and day by day, the old Jen started to re-emerge. I stopped feeling so ashamed of how I had been feeling. It was only then that I started to realise how much I was missing out on. I loved my daughter more than anything; my recovery didn't mean I loved her more, it meant I enjoyed her more.

Future Pregnancies

I did worry that postnatal depression would return if I had more children. I worried that people might judge me for having more children when I had struggled with depression after my first, but more than anything I knew I didn't want postnatal depression to prevent me from having more children.

Whilst pregnant with my second child I asked to be referred to the hospital psychiatrist. He proved to be an enormous help, speaking with me not only about the depression I had experienced but also about the miscarriage that had preceded this pregnancy. He listened and questioned and helped me to come up with a plan for after the birth of the baby I was carrying.

I've never been one to just sit back and be told what to do. In many ways I'm a doctor's worst nightmare I imagine. I like to research and question most things that I'm told, not with the intention of being difficult but because I like to be properly informed. I find it impossible to follow advice blindly; I need to be actively involved.

I mentioned some research I had come across to the psychiatrist, which suggested that there may be some benefits to a woman taking a low dose of antidepressant medication immediately following the birth of her baby. A 'prevention is better than cure' approach. It was ironic considering how much I battled against taking medication the first time around but I was desperate not to repeat the experience. The psychiatrist agreed that this might be a good option for me and so it was the route we took. Whether I can attribute it to my avoiding postnatal depression that time or not I don't know, but it didn't return. I was seen by the psychiatrist again a few days after my eldest son's birth and I don't think I've ever been happier. In spite of a difficult birth, my life was absolutely perfect.

I'd love to say I found a magic cure and this was the solution to keeping postnatal depression at bay, but it turned out this was only time I managed to avoid it. On each other occasion the depression returned shortly after my babies' births. It always manifested itself in a similar manner. I couldn't bear to be separated from my babies or their siblings. Crazy as it might sound, even a trip to do the grocery shopping without all my children in tow often ended with me in tears, convinced that the other shoppers would think that I was a bad mum for not taking all of my children with me. It didn't matter that they were safely at home with their dad. It didn't matter that the other shoppers didn't know me and therefore had no clue how many children I did or didn't have. It didn't matter that I was surrounded by stressed-out parents who were too busy haring it up and down the aisles after energetic toddlers with destruction on their minds to even notice me. I judged me so I assumed everyone else did too.

What Helped Me

Familiarity should have meant that I knew what to do to help myself recover the second and subsequent times but my reluctance to take medication meant I often let things go further than they should have before seeking help. Counselling was an outlet I also tried, but with little or no childcare support attending was a challenge in itself.

If I could go back in time and give one piece of advice to myself it would be to go to the doctor sooner rather than later. My GP was amazing and had an ability to reason with me in a way that I couldn't reason with myself. He assured me when it happened subsequent times that I would get better, that I knew I would because I had before. He reminded me that I could continue as I was but the reality was that I was making these weeks and months more difficult for myself than they needed to be.

He reassured me that I could continue to breastfeed as my medication would be tapered to suit and that was a huge thing for me. If you have postnatal depression and you want to stop breastfeeding then that is absolutely the correct decision, but if you have postnatal depression and you don't want to stop, then stopping could make it worse. I feel that if I had had to stop it would have tipped me over the edge, another perceived failure on my part.

I was also reminded that there were some things I had to do and some things I didn't need to do. I needed to try to do things that had previously brought me pleasure but I didn't need to attend events that would only stress me further. I needed to be with my children until I felt better in myself and happier to leave the house without some, or all, of them. I needed to be kind to myself and allow myself to recover in the same way that I would allow myself to recover from a physical ailment.

I remained until now always very private about my experiences. I never confided in anyone while I was suffering, although I spoke more freely with very close friends and family once I felt better. The privacy was partly because of the shame I felt and partly because of vulnerability. Stigma still surrounds mental health issues, in spite of efforts to dispel it. As a mother of beautiful, healthy children I felt I had no right to feel the way I did. One person even said to me that I 'wasn't the only woman ever to have had a baby'. Now, of course, I can appreciate that this was a thoughtless and ignorant comment but at the time I thought the person was right, and it compounded my sense of failure.

Talking is generally a good idea though and I was surprised by the amount of people who had been through the same thing. The midwife at one of my antenatal registration visits shared her experience of postnatal depression with me as she entered my details into the hospital computer system. It was a reminder that even the experts in all things pregnancy- and baby-related are not immune to it.

All in all, it was the combined effects of taking the prescribed medication, talking to those I could trust and trying to re-involve myself in the things I had always enjoyed, at my own pace, that made the greatest difference to my recovery. Seeking help sooner rather than later is the key. And know that you will feel better and, horrid though the experience may be while you're going through it, it will change you for the better too. It will bring you a new level of empathy and understanding that you never before knew. It will help you to appreciate the fragility of mental health and truly understand that mental health issues can affect anyone. It will make you appreciate the need to look after yourself and you will learn one of life's lessons when it comes to what's truly important.

4

RETURN TO WORK OR STAY AT HOME?

To the inexperienced, maternity leave can appear like a fantastic chunk of time stretching out in front of you, during which you'll get to know baby, go for plenty of walks in the park, have lazy, relaxed coffees, get involved in the whole 'mother-and-baby scene' and get some of that long-overdue home decorating done.

Once baby arrives, of course, the days and nights run into each other, as do the days and weeks, and managing to have a shower and get dressed become the new goals rather than wallpapering the sitting room. But, as the passing of time gathers pace and maternity leave gallops towards its end, decisions need to be made about whether to return to work or stay at home.

In the same manner in which the reality of your maternity leave experiences can prove very different to your expectations, many of your pre-baby ideals and plans may change after baby's birth. A baby can change our perspective completely. Some formerly career-oriented women may suddenly find themselves breaking out in a sweat at the thought of leaving their babies with a stranger and all plans are turned on their heads. Others, who may have thought a stay-at-home mum's life might suit them perfectly, now find themselves counting down the days until their return to work, where they can use the bathroom with the door closed and possibly even finish a cup of coffee in one sitting.

What's perfect for one is not necessarily so for another and we all must do what suits our own family dynamic best. Nonetheless, working-outside-the-home mums and stay-at-home mums can sometimes find themselves pitted against each other, with a lack of real appreciation but plenty of judgement when it comes to the others' choices. The reality is we all do what we think is best for our own family unit and operate within our own personal constraints. There is a lot to consider and factor in before making a final decision on the road you plan to take – if that decision is even in your hands.

RETURNING TO WORK

There is no real optimum time to return to work and how long you can manage to stay at home with your baby will vary from individual to individual. Unpaid maternity leave is a statutory entitlement but the 'unpaid' element means that it may not be an option for everyone. Your child's age may also have an impact, depending on when your childcare provider is prepared to accept them.

While our choices are often bound by the confines of what our pocket can afford and the flexibility we require, there may be some options open to you that can help to make the transition a little easier.

Full-Time or Part-Time

Returning to work full-time can feel a little overwhelming when it comes to juggling the demands of home life and work life, but an alternative may not be available. The big advantage of working full-time is obviously the full-time wage. Childcare costs are obviously more, but to my surprise I discovered that part-time childcare is not always proportionately cheaper.

Returning to work offers an outlet too. It can be a break from the isolation, and a return to a place where you are still you, and not just mum. It can be an opportunity to return to a job that you possibly love and that makes you feel fulfilled. It can give you back a sense of independence. Or it can be plain old lack of choice, with bills to play and inflexible working options.

I was fortunate enough that following the birth of my first child my employer allowed me to work on a part-time basis immediately upon my return from maternity leave. It had always been my hope to work part-time once I had children, but my initial plan was to work-share on a split week basis – three days one week, two days another. In my pre-baby days that seemed the best option to me and the prospect of full days at home with my baby was very appealing. Once my daughter arrived however and I considered the very long days that she was facing in childcare, due to the fact that I worked in a different county to which I lived, I changed my mind and opted for the mornings-only option.

It's often described as the best of both of both worlds and some days it is. Other days it's the worst of both worlds. Mornings only means that I'm there for the morning chaos, I run out the door to work, leave at lunchtime (without having had lunch), return home to a house that looks as if it has been ransacked by burglars – merely a result of trying to get everybody out the door and to where they should be on time – and then the school collections and homework delights begin.

Somewhere in between trying to put the house back together again, play with the little ones, break up the older ones' arguments, manage homework battles, get to the shops for random 'must haves by tomorrow', do several loads of washing, bring and collect my children from afterschool activities and prepare dinner for everyone, I try to fit in a luke-warm cup of tea and a sandwich – actually usually just bread and butter because there's often not time to cut some cheese. The children, eternally grateful as children tend to be, generally manage to forget that I've been to work at all.

On the plus side, mornings only help hugely with mammy guilt. I'm lucky enough to be there to oversee those aforementioned homework battles and being at home every afternoon means that, as long as I don't object to being a constant mum-taxi, I'm not as restricted when it comes to the times of afterschool activities. I can also plan the children's doctors' and dental appointments for the afternoon and parent–teacher meetings can be scheduled around my work timetable too. I'm also lucky enough to be there so that I can arrange playdates for my children.

Of course not everyone has the option of working part-time but a statutory entitlement to parental leave for both parents means that reducing the length of your working week may be an option for a period at least. Part-time workers are also entitled to avail of parental leave on a pro-rata basis. The manner in which parental leave can be taken is varied and some patterns are at the discretion of your employer, so it's definitely worth speaking to them about your preferred option. Nothing ventured, nothing gained.

Working from home can be another option for some mothers, removing the need for a commute and saving valuable and precious time on certain days. Depending on your employer and your line of work, remote access may make this a possibility. It won't remove the need for childcare but it might result in a slightly less chaotic morning rush and, without the need to travel, the end of your working day means your home life can commence immediately.

It's not always as idyllic as it might sound though. It can be difficult to separate and maintain the boundaries between home life and work life when home and office are the same. Even others' perceptions of you working from home can be askew, with a misplaced belief that you're fitting in some work around running the home.

Working from home requires a high degree of organisation and planning and a reiterating to family, friends and even partners sometimes that you are actually working and not necessarily available to fit in children's various appointments, personal phone calls or childcare duties at the drop of a hat. But if you can get the balance right, it can be the perfect solution for some.

Breastfeeding and Working

For breastfeeding mums, returning to work – whether full-time or part-time – needn't mean an end to their breastfeeding days. All breastfeeding mums have a statutory entitlement to breastfeeding breaks for a period (currently until baby is six months old) and these entitlements are applied on a pro-rata basis for part-time workers. The manner in which these breaks are taken can be arranged with your employer, with some employees preferring to spread their breaks throughout the working day and others preferring to finish work earlier. Unfortunately the difficulty with this timeframe is that by the time most women return to work the statutory entitlement will have lapsed. Some employers, however, including the civil service, extend the period of entitlement beyond the statutory limits, reflecting the World Health Organisation's recommendation that a child be breastfed until the age of two or beyond.

It's worth speaking with your employer ahead of your return to see what their policy is and to discuss your options, if any. Even if your employer doesn't allow for an extended period, it may still be possible to continue to feed your baby in the morning and evening time and express at lunchtime for your comfort – and future supplies for the childminder. Your body and milk supply will adjust quickly and accordingly. If pumping is not an option for you, depending on your child's age food and water and alternative milk may suffice. Many children simply reverse their pattern of feeding when a mum returns to work and will feed more in the evening time instead. Breastfeeding your child when you pick them up after work can be a lovely way to reconnect.

Childcare

Childcare costs can be almost prohibitive in terms of returning to work, ruling out the option completely for some and making it barely worthwhile for others. Cost, however, as significant a factor as it may be, is just the tip of the iceberg when trying to decide on your preferred type of childcare. Flexibility, proximity to home and work, what will happen if your child is ill and the situation regarding any other children you may have play equally important roles. Every childcare option has its advantages and disadvantages. Trying to work out the one that will suit you best is the hardest part.

Crèche

For many people a crèche is the ideal childcare solution and the advantages of crèche-based childcare are easy to see:

- Fully trained staff
- Many provide almost year-round cover
- No worries about your childcare provider becoming ill and unable to take care of your child
- The company of other children and plenty of child-based activities which can progress as your child grows
- Many crèches operate a collection service to and from local schools. This means if you have school-going children, childcare can all be sourced from the same childcare provider without your child needing to go on school runs, or other trips, with their carer.

The disadvantages however include:

- Frequent illness for your child as germs spread rapidly amongst groups of children
- Little opportunity for one-on-one time for your child which can be particularly difficult if your child is shy or nervous
- Inconsistency in carers as the crèche relocate staff to other areas of the facility and your child moves through the different age groups and to different 'rooms' (e.g. baby, wobbler, toddler rooms)
- Cost can a big factor here, especially if you have more than one child attending a crèche.
- Lack of flexibility with regards to opening and closing times can prove very problematic if a long commute to work is involved or you don't work typical 9–5 hours.

Childminder

For those who would prefer a more homely childcare environment, a childminder is often the obvious choice. With a childminder the advantages include:

- A consistency in childcare with the same person looking after your child each day. This can be of great comfort to a nervous or shy child in particular.
- The consistency in childcare means that the childminder is more likely to spot any out of character behaviour in your child, which enables them to flag concerns to you if they feel your child might be upset or ill.
- Depending on the policy of the childminder, and sometimes whether the childminder takes care of your child in your home or theirs, it may be possible for the childminder to take care of your child while your child has a minor illness such as a cold, for example.
- Sometimes a childminder is a more affordable option.
- Your child may be taken care of in a family environment.
- There's more opportunity for one-on-one time.
- There may be more flexibility around working hours.

The disadvantages however can include:

- A lack of back-up if your childminder becomes ill
- A childminder's holidays are usually more than the amount of time a crèche closes in a year.
- Your child may have no other children to play with.
- Alternatively, your child may have to fit around your childminder's daily life which may include the collection of her own or other children she takes care of, regardless of the weather.

Family

More and more grandparents are becoming involved in the provision of childcare for their grandchildren. You only have to look around you at the school gates and chances are you'll see almost as many grandparents there at pick-up time as parents. Often providing the ultimate solution in terms of reduced costs and additional flexibility, having a family member take care of your baby or child can make the return to work a little easier. Knowing that the person taking care of your precious bundle has a vested interest and truly loves them is a huge comfort. Chances are a family member will also be familiar with how you 'do' things and the child has the added benefit of already knowing their carer.

But, like everything, it comes with its own cost. As grateful as you may be for the invaluable childcare that your family may provide, a professional relationship is impossible. There are many things that you may have to let go when a family member is also your child-minder, things that you might address otherwise.

Adoring relations may have very different views as to how much junk food, TV/electronics time, and so on is acceptable. They may not insist that homework is carried out to your standards. They may relax boundaries that you have set for your child or they may impose more stringent ones. You may even be treated to a rendition of 'it didn't do you any harm.' You can voice your opinion, gently of course, but the lack of professional relationship means it may not be heard and you may have to just 'suck it up' and get on with it.

Au Pair

Au pairs have been steadily growing in popularity as a childcare option for people who would prefer to have their children taken care of in their own home. The flexibility can be very appealing but there are a lot of other things that need to be considered.

Au pairs are generally young women (and men) who come to the country in the hope of improving their level of English. Many of them have little or no childcare experience and while they can be of invaluable assistance as a mother's help, often au pairs are not a suitable option when it comes to taking sole care of a baby or very young child. For parents who work outside the home, an au pair is probably a more suitable option for those who work part-time rather than full-time.

It's important not to underestimate the adjustment period involved as you become the au pair's new family and they settle into your household, in a new country, and get to know the dynamic.

Living with another person can be challenging and the surrender of a bedroom a huge deal if you're already tight for space.

The language barrier requires careful consideration also, particularly if your child is to be left in the sole care of the au pair periodically. How will they communicate, especially if there is a difficulty or, worse still, an emergency?

The lack of consistency can be unsettling for children. Au pairs can come for different lengths of time and in an ideal situation they build up a wonderful relationship with your family; the hard part for your children is when they leave. Best-laid plans aren't always realised however, and sometimes, no matter how wonderful the relationship is, job or study opportunities can arise in the au pair's home country which can see them needing to leave sooner than anticipated. Then there are the times when you spoke to Mary Poppins via Skype, but Cruella De Vil disembarked the plane and once again you're back to the drawing board.

When you meet the right au pair, however, they can be a wonderful addition to a family, teaching you about their culture as well as learning about yours and, if you're lucky, remaining a family friend for years to come, long after they've returned home.

There is no one size fits all when it comes to childcare options and even an apparent ideal solution may need to change as your child grows and your family possibly grows too. All that any of us can do is make the decision that suits us best at the time of making and see how things pan out.

Making Working Outside the Home Work for You

Juggling everything is hard. Time is precious and can seem in very short supply when you're trying to manage it all. Organisation is the key and even the most disorganised of us have to get involved in some degree of planning. In addition to taking the stress out of already hectic days, it will allow you to maximise and take advantage of any time that you have available and make sure that you're in the best place possible for when the unexpected inevitably strikes.

- Leave out all clothes and shoes for the next day – always. Don't be tempted to skip this step. Sod's law will dictate that one of your toddler's favourite shoes will have disappeared from the face of the earth if you try to and won't turn up until all manner of tantrums have taken place, yours included. Cue the day being off to a bad start.
- Prepare lunches the night before if possible. It's one less thing to do the next morning.
- When you're making dinner, if you can, make extra and freeze it for another day. You'll be so grateful that you did in the evening time. Plan your meals for the week, rather than wasting time when you come home wondering what to cook and realising that you don't have all the ingredients you need.
- Have the children's school bags/childcare bags packed and ready to go, notes signed and any monies required for the next day ready in an envelope. Top tip: once you have school-aged children always have change available for buying copies, pencils, tin whistles, etc.
- Get up before your children and get ready before they're awake, no matter how tired you are. It's hard to predict how any morning will go, or how cranky various members of the family will be. You may need more time than anticipated for cajoling kids along and clearing up spilled orange juice as the two-year-old attempts to recreate a 'jumping up and down in muddy puddles' scene.
- Remember to take time out for you. Tired as you may be after the week's demands, try to have an outlet: meet with friends, go to an exercise class, return to a hobby. Do something that you enjoy and that is separate from the demands of being a work-outside-the-home mum. Keeping the ship afloat requires the captain to be in the best state of health, physically and emotionally, that she possibly can be.
- Go to bed at a reasonable time. Sounds like a given, but the temptation to stay up too late is real, especially when the day has been manic. Chill certainly, but get adequate rest.
- Let it go. A bad morning or evening is just that. On a day when a child-sized universe seems to be working against you and, in

the efforts to get everything done and get everyone where they need to be, there's been more raised voices and tears than you ever thought possible, let it go and put it behind you. Tomorrow is another day and things will hopefully be better.

STAYING AT HOME

Becoming a stay-at-home mum isn't always a matter of choice. Sometimes the cost of childcare can exceed your earning potential. Sometimes the demands at home are too much to practically consider returning to the workforce, and sometimes an adequately flexible childcare solution is not available.

Sometimes it is a choice however, but that doesn't mean that there isn't a fallout. Financially it can be tough learning to survive without an additional income, and the upside of having that extra time with your child can result in the need for significant financial sacrifices.

After the birth of my fourth child, I took a career break from work. The demands at home, a commute to my older children's school and the cost of childcare meant that staying at home was the most practical option for me at the time. Few things drove me crazier than flippant remarks such as 'isn't it well for you who can afford to stay at home?' The reality was more that I couldn't afford to work.

My own work-sharing pattern meant that I never had more than two children in childcare at any one time, as the older children were in school while I was at work. But, as childcare costs rose at a much faster rate than my salary, staying at home was a no brainer. I was very grateful to have the opportunity to stay at home with my children, even though the loss of a wage meant that I debated all purchases, only buying what was absolutely essential rather than desired. Even my definition of 'absolutely essential' changed.

I thought that maternity leave had prepared me somewhat for the challenges that staying at home would present. The reality of my maternity leaves, however, were that I continued to keep my childcare options available to me, even if I didn't use them all of the time, because I knew that I would need them again once I returned to work. The surrender of that back-up when I took my career break meant that baby check-ups, for one, no longer involved just me and my baby, but also required heroic escapades and rescue efforts on my part when it came to saving the goldfish in the doctor's waiting room from my accompanying two-year-old.

When school shows and cake sales came around, the requirement to take a day off work was replaced with the challenge of trying to find someone to take care of my toddler and prevent a stage invasion or a mass clearance of products that were on sale. I realised that I never valued my ability to time a dental appointment, if necessary, with a day's leave while my children who were not yet at school were taken care of by their minder. I may have been freer in theory once I became a stay-at-home mum, but the prospect of attending the dentist with the littles in tow means you start to evaluate your pain differently.

Making Staying at Home Work for You

Maternity leave prepares you for some aspects of staying at home and chances are that it may have given you some insight into the levels of isolation that can be involved. If you decide to be a stay-at-home parent, it's more important than ever to continue to involve yourself in activities that see you meeting other people. One of the advantages of being a stay-at-home mum is the opportunity to meet other stay-at-home mums on the school and Montessori drops, if you have children of that age. They can be great beacons of knowledge, up to speed on all the mother-and-child activities in the locality and full of advice as to how to get your 'grown-up fix'.

Online outlets and parenting forums are great and have their place in supporting mums on their parenting journey, but in this age of technology there's a danger of becoming over-reliant on virtual friends. In the long run, the virtual world is not likely to offer you enough in terms of company, so be careful not to fall into the trap of having online friends only and instead make a real effort to meet real people.

Working outside the home creates a structure for us – not necessarily one of our liking but a structure nonetheless. The advantage of being at home means that you can tailor a structure that suits you better, but do make sure to tailor one. Schedule time for going with the flow, but schedule time for getting out and getting the things done that you need to do. The day, busy as it is, can seem endless without any plans. Without the escapism and camaraderie of work coffee break time, it can feel like it's all slog and no play.

Especially on days where it all feels a little bit thankless, remind yourself of the practical advantages – of which there are many. In addition to having the ability to spend more time with your children, you won't have the stress of trying to juggle work with a sick child or children. The vomiting bug, aka the plague, hit our home several months ago, taking down six of the children in its grip. As we drowned in vomit and endless washing, somewhere, deep inside me, a Pollyanna-like sentiment rose to the surface and I was grateful for the fact that I was still on maternity leave. I don't actually know how I would have managed in terms of taking time off work had I not been. The children fell afoul of the plague in staggered sequence of course, for maximum disruption, so I would have needed at least two weeks off work for that dose alone.

There's also the quandary of school and Montessori holidays to factor in – and there are plenty of them. Add to the equation the extra days off that schoolchildren often get around bank holidays and earlier finishing times because of parent–teacher meetings, etc. and the whole work–life balance can really be tested. As a stay-at-home mum, these issues are less of a worry. Yes you may be driven to levels of distraction that you never thought possible when you're at home all day with children who keep asking 'What are we doing now? What are we doing now?', but at least you won't be forced into having to sign up for some expensive camps just to resolve the childcare dilemma – unless you want to of course.

Many years ago a mum who stayed at home with her children told me that one of the biggest annoyances for her and difficulties that she struggled with, when she first decided to stay at home, was the belief of many working mums in her circle that she would be available at the drop of a hat to rescue a child whose childminder hadn't turned up, to take care of a child whose parents were delayed at work or to collect a child whose mother had received a phone call from the school or crèche to say that their little one was ill. And so it came to pass that I realised she was absolutely spot on.

Feeling taken for granted is horrible. The assumption that you're always there and 'sure what else would you be doing anyway?' can be hard to take. Emergencies aside, don't be afraid to say no if it doesn't suit you – and some days it really won't. Helping out is great, if you're in a position to do so, but if the requests start to become a little too frequent don't be afraid to explain that, actually, you have something going on that day and you won't always be able to help. It's not an easy thing to do, but your frustrations will just build if it continues to happen over and over and over again.

Taking up a non-mum-related hobby can really help with supporting the part of you that's you, not mum. That's not to say that your hobby can't involve mum friends, but it shouldn't be about being a mum. The role of a stay-at-home mum is all-consuming. There are no set hours, no annual leave and toilet breaks are rarely unaccompanied. Home and office are one and the same and, thanks to a lack of teeth, the company over coffee often needs their food pureed, so the potential topics for conversation are limited.

A non-mum hobby lets you be you again, and to the people with whom you share your hobby you are you, not mum. Being a stay-at-home mum can sometimes mean that you feel your sense of identity start to disappear. Involving yourself in an adult activity outside of the home not only helps you to feel like you again but has the added bonus of people using your actual name. A hobby or activity gives you a break from one of the most tiring roles you'll ever have. Privilege as it may be to have all this time with your children, it's absolutely exhausting, and we all need a break and an opportunity to recharge the batteries.

Mum Guilt

Rest assured, no matter what choices you make in any and every aspect of parenthood, mum guilt will rear its head, making you feel just downright rotten sometimes, even when what you've done or what you're doing is for the best. This seemingly pointless emotion is borne of adoration and manages to hold all of us in its tight grip while we grapple with feelings of inadequacy and question our judgement.

While mum guilt may have existed since the dawn of time, social media and its many platforms means we're subjected to daily images of picture-perfect family scenes where children and adults alike all beam gaily at the camera, reflecting their perfect, non-snot-filled, non-tantrum-throwing lives. Clothes are all perfectly coordinated, not a hair is out of place and there are no signs of baby puke on mum's clothes. The sun even seems to make an appearance for the occasion. You, meanwhile, are chasing your bare-bottomed eighteen-month-old around the sitting room, after his three-year-old brother removed his poo-filled nappy while you dared to take ten seconds out to visit the bathroom. Naturally enough, the contents of that same nappy are everywhere, having been trodden in by the same bare-bottomed eighteen-month-old and evidence of the path he took is all over your once brightly coloured mat in the hall. It's probably not a picture that you'd choose to show on social media – but it is real life, and it is actually mine.

Social media rarely tells the full story. It won't tell of the battles that may have taken place before that perfect picture was realised. It won't tell you if their house has been left in a catastrophic state, such were the efforts to actually get out the door. It won't tell you if mum is worried about some aspect of her child's development and it won't tell you if mum is still full of smiles when the camera isn't looking.

Motherhood is held up as a holy grail of perfection. As celebrities gush about how motherhood completes them and happily pose for the professional photographers, having had their hair styled and make-up expertly applied by the professionals, and had the nanny watch their children in the interim, an unrealistic view of parenthood continues to be portrayed. Of course it's not just celebrities. The mums at the school gate, in your office, at the crèche or at your mother-and-toddler group can all be selective about the aspects of parenthood they discuss and the details they choose to share.

As the unrealistic expectations exist and the fear of being perceived a failure in any or all aspects of the most important job ever remain, the vicious cycle continues.

Mum guilt can be applied to so many areas of parenthood, and we all have our particular sensitivities and individual things that we worry about most. Working outside the home or becoming a stay-at-home mother, however, is one of the aspects that most of us fret about. Mums who work outside the home can feel guilty and worry that they might miss a precious and important first. Let me reassure you on this one – being at home is no guarantee you'll witness a 'first' anyhow. My daughter decided to take her first, eagerly awaited, much anticipated, camcorder-at-the-ready step on a Saturday, when I had no work. Problem was I had gone to the shops, and so she took her first steps for her grandparents and uncle, who incidentally weren't camcorder-ready. I got to see the many more steps that followed, but for a period I cursed that litre of milk and coffee cake I went to buy.

It's not just missing firsts, of course, that can trigger mum guilt. Potential long hours in childcare, the possibility of missing school shows and cake sales, an inability to do the school run, or the impossible practicalities of playdates can all add to a working mum's guilt.

Stay-at-home mums, meanwhile, can feel guilty for not setting an example for their daughters in particular, for not being seen to 'have it all'. Some stay-at-home mums can feel guilt for not making a perceived active enough contribution to society (because taking care of tomorrow's adults is not sufficient it seems) or for not being able to afford the material luxuries and holidays that another possibly might.

Real and overwhelming at times as the guilt can feel, it's rarely justified. We all make our decisions based on the information we have and the place we are at that time. We do what we think is best for us, for our family as a unit and for each individual child. While mum guilt can be a motivator to correct something within our power that really doesn't sit well with us, it shouldn't be used as a stick to beat ourselves with. Some choices are not ours to make and some things would happen irrespective of the decisions we do take.

Mums are people too – real-life human beings, beneath their invisible cape. Sometimes we get it right, sometimes we get it wrong and sometimes we need to prioritise our own needs just that tiny little bit. Happy mum equals happy baby/child. What bigger motivator could we need?

Tips for Overcoming Mum Guilt

- Put a bad day behind you and start afresh.
- Give yourself due credit when you've got something right.
- Be reasonable with yourself about what is achievable.
- Keep things in perspective. We all shout sometimes, even though we shouldn't. Stop, say sorry, regroup and carry on.
- Try to accept what you cannot change. Make the best of it and don't dwell on it. Some things are simply out of your control.
- Remind yourself that no one has your child's best interests at heart more than you.

In trying to manage the whole mum guilt conundrum, remember that you only feel as you do because of the intensity of love that you have for your child – and they love you too. They're not looking for the superhuman, unachievable perfection that you strive for. They love you just the way you are, normalities and all. To them, you're already perfect.

5

THE TODDLER AND THREENAGER YEARS

Somewhere, roughly around the eighteen-month-old mark – possibly a little before, possibly a little after – your once tiny, helpless baby will change from being an agreeable, generally compliant baby (who doesn't sleep) to an especially energetic, furniture-scaling, whirlwind force of nature (who in my case still doesn't sleep).

The smiles remain, but a newfound glint of mischief can be seen in the eyes of this pint-sized terror for whom safety gates are an obstacle merely to be overcome and whose favourite word now is 'No' – not a gentle, room-for-negotiation type 'no', but more of a 'dream on, it's not happening without a fight' type 'NO!'

The toddler and threenager years are filled with new milestones, met at varied and individual rates, new challenges and the emergence of a strong sense of identity. In their eyes, though most probably not yours, they're no longer babies, but indeed 'big boys' and 'big girls', capable of doing things for themselves, at a sometimes painstakingly slow speed. They have an opinion, they have an attitude – and they're not afraid to use them.

The world for toddlers is a place to be explored, with little regard for their own safety. Their newfound mobility means most things are now within reach with a little furniture manoeuvring. Everything is of interest, particularly things they've been told are dangerous or dirty, and as for speed – never underestimate the speed with which a determined toddler can operate. And so, just as you thought you were getting a handle on parenthood, and getting your head around the endless amount of baby paraphernalia that now litters your house, you realise it's time to find a new home for all of your precious trinkets before they're relocated for you. Your home is under toddler attack. Resistance is futile. It's an exercise of damage limitation.

TODDLER-PROOFING YOUR HOME

When my daughter was born, my neighbour's mother popped in to have a look, to congratulate me and to pass on some words of wisdom: 'Enjoy this stage, this is the easy part', she said. In my sleep-deprived, milk-leaking, stitch-hurting, highly emotional state I figured she was quite obviously barmy, so I nodded at her in a near sympathetic manner.

Everything's relative of course, and what she really meant, though I'm sure I still probably wouldn't have appreciated it at the time, was that one of the joys of a very young baby is that they generally stay where you put them. If a very young baby is placed on their playmat and you run to answer the door, baby is still there when you come back. If the heavens open and you run to save the washing that you put out three days ago but still haven't had the chance to take back in yet, such are the demands of new parenthood, and you place baby securely in their bouncer, you can rest safe in the knowledge that baby will still be there when you come back indoors again.

As the weeks and months pass though, and celebrations follow those first rollovers and, in time, that first crawl or bum-shuffle, popping anywhere, no matter how briefly, becomes a bit more of a challenge. In line with the growing ability to 'get places', Houdini-like escape artist skills also begin to develop. In due course, trips to the bathroom and taking a shower alone become distant memories, as no solace can be taken from the fact that your toddler is asleep at that moment in time. The sides of the cot are a mere baby-climbing frame, to be scaled with ease – though the descent needs some work.

And so the time comes to toddler-proof your home. Danger lurks everywhere for the inquisitive child and while trips to A&E can be necessary in spite of our best efforts, prevention is better than cure, always.

Safety Equipment

- Corner protectors for tables are a must-have. Toddlers have a wonderful tendency to run with their heads down, and even when they don't, their brakes aren't very efficient or effective. Heads and eyes are particularly vulnerable as toddlers are the perfect height for table collisions. The protectors might not prevent them running into the tables but should help lessen the impact. Corner protectors are a great idea for fireplace corners too.

- Socket protectors are another essential. After many months of watching you use the sockets for the hoover, hairdryer, phone chargers and the like, a mobile toddler is just waiting to see what happens if they stick a pencil, a finger or other random objects into it. Be warned, however, some socket protectors are so effective that it's not just children who will find them difficult to remove – as is the case with the ones I used in a low-down double socket in my kitchen. We haven't been able to access it since the birth of my fifth child.

- Drawer, press and fridge locks are very important in not only protecting tiny little fingers from damage but also in preventing toddlers from accessing potentially dangerous sharp knives or heavy tins which cause a lot of pain and damage if they fall on precious little toes.

- The idea of a toilet lock can seem like a huge inconvenience, but after your phone ends up down the toilet for the third time you'll begin to appreciate its benefits. All manner of things can go down the loo when you have young children in the house. Once your child is past the age of four it's generally an accidental occurrence. Before that age, however, a toilet appears to have a magnet-like draw for toddlers and they can feel an overwhelming desire to put anything – anything in their hands, anything within a six feet radius of them, or anything that normally resides in the kitchen – down it. A threenager may attempt to fish the offending item out with a toothbrush. A toddler will normally just chuck the toothbrush down the toilet too.

For this reason, a good rule of thumb when you have a toddler in the house is to check the toilet for missing objects. Car keys, several mobile phones, the television remote control, a Peter Kay DVD, and numerous breakfast waffles have all met their watery end at the bottom of our toilet bowl.

- Safety clips for blind and curtain cords. These are just a non-negotiable essential with small children in the house. Cords should be kept taut and out of children's reach at all times and a child's cot never placed in a position that might facilitate more easy access.

- Stairgates are needed as soon as baby is mobile and are required at both the top and bottom of your staircase. They can also be used between doorways to restrict access to certain rooms. You'll need lots of patience with them. While they're very easy to install, unless you secure them to the wall older children and absent-minded partners will step on them as they walk through and bring them crashing down, frequently. They have also been known to trap unsuspecting grandparents who are not familiar with double-locking systems.

About the House

By their very nature, a toddler can make anything dangerous. Trying to spot the hazard before your toddler does is the challenge:

- Chairs – the kitchen and dining-room type – are easy to move for a strong-willed toddler and a mere stepping stone to danger. We have had to resort to stacking our chairs on top of our tables, such has been the determination of our toddlers. On countless occasions, prior to this practice, we discovered the toddler dancing his version of head, shoulders, knees and toes on our dining-room table, somewhat oblivious to edges and the drop he faced should he put a foot wrong. The chairs also enabled easy access to the light switches, which were turned on, and off, and on and off and on again – this game never seems to get boring.

Chairs have also been used to gain access to mantelpieces and kitchen counters, and on one occasion a quick interception was required as one particular toddler attempted to escape out the sitting-room window to visit his dog. Nowhere is inaccessible to a toddler if there's a chair in sight. While stacking them on the table when you've finished eating has an essence of schooldays about it, the comparative peace that you'll have in the long run is worth it.

- Choking hazards and poisons – so many things can fall into this category but there are some things a toddler will naturally be drawn to. Coins are one, especially if they've ever seen or tasted the chocolate variety before. Toddlers can be destructive little creatures too, so be careful to take note of any toys with moveable or potentially removable-by-force pieces.

  Anything brightly coloured is likely to catch their eye. Bleach may be an obvious danger but colourful dishwasher and detergent capsules that can resemble large sweets or jellies are also something to be aware of. As for medicines, grateful as we may be of their lovely sweet taste when trying to encourage a reluctant and poorly toddler to take some, that same taste means a child will be drawn to them when they're well too. Childproof caps are great, but out of sight, out of mind is definitely the best policy.

- Indoor keys – the easiest thing here is to remove them. There is usually no advance warning that a toddler has mastered the art of key turning until they've locked themselves in a room. Be mindful of keys when you visit other people's houses too. It's easy to forget that in non-toddler households people are used to being able to lock the bathroom door.

- Chests of drawers and storage units – these need to be secured to the walls. Toddlers and small children love to climb, and unsecured these can cause serious injury or even death. The weight of several drawers open at the same time can lead the chest or storage unit to topple, even without a climber.

- Cot bedding and cuddly toys – while adorable fluffy bedding, pillows and teddies can make your toddler's bed look very cosy and appealing, they can be used to assist your little one with a middle-of-the-night or early-morning escape. In your toddler's eagerness to be reunited with you, the contents of the cot can be used to build a platform to facilitate a bid for freedom. Getting down the other side can prove the real difficulty though and bring a whole new meaning to the phrase 'things that go bump in the night'.

Of course it's not just in matters of personal safety that toddlers and indeed threenagers keep us on our toes. As their personalities continue to emerge and their newfound voice and speech continues to develop, you can find yourself subject to their frustrations, upset and blatant repeating of something you said at the most inopportune of times.

OUT OF THE MOUTHS OF BABES

'Be careful what you say in front on them' and 'they're like sponges, they take it all in' were just two of the many pieces of advice I was offered when I first became a mum. It proved to be excellent advice. If you think back to the games of peek-a-boo and round-and-round-the-garden that you played with baby and recall your delight when baby moved on from just laughing to actually imitating you and actively participating, you'll see that all the signs were there. All the warning signs that your clever little baby was taking it all in, and throwing it back out. And yet, chances are, unless you have incredibly impressive resolve, you will have slipped up somewhere along the way, and used the sort of language that you would prefer your child didn't repeat.

You may also have passed a flippant comment to your partner about a neighbour who has annoyed you (or worse still a family member) and you may have thought no more of it. Whether or not your toddler or threenager thought no more of it though tends to come to light within about two minutes of meeting the person in question – and unfortunately the incubation period is unpredictable.

My daughter was the first to teach us about a toddler's sponge-like tendencies. As my husband drove her home from Montessori one day, a car pulled out in front of him. My hubby beeped the horn, muttered something to himself, and continued driving. Moments later, a little voice called out from the back seat. 'I'm telling Mum', the voice said. 'You said a bad word.' As my husband tried to recall exactly which bad word he had used, he realised that he was going to need some prompting. 'I don't think I did, honey', he protested. 'You did', she replied. 'It was the bad word beginning with "O".' By now my husband was completely stumped. In spite of knowing many bad words, he couldn't, for the life of him, think of any that began with 'O'. 'I think you'll need to tell me love', he said. 'I don't know any bad words that begin with "O", maybe you made a mistake.' 'You called that man an Orsehole', my daughter replied. The mature and appropriate response here of course would have been to point out that Daddy was wrong, that this was not a nice thing to say, and this was not a nice word to use. The actual response included much snorting and hysterical laughter while the adamant three-year-old maintained her stern and critical composure. Much later, when Daddy had finally regained his, the appropriate response was given.

And that was about as bad as it got, for a time. We never really had an issue with 'undesirable' language with any of the children, in spite of the odd slip-up in front of them – until child number six came along. Child six learned to speak quite quickly. He had many teachers in his siblings and progressed quickly from 'mama' and 'dada' to naming his sister and brothers and his beloved dog. Every character in *Ben and Holly's Little Kingdom* and *Peppa Pig* quickly followed. He informed us that 'magic always leads to trouble' and that if you're going to 'jump up and down in muddy puddles, you must wear your boots'.

And others understood him outside of the family too, which isn't always the case with toddlers. He could communicate clearly, relatively speaking of course, and everyone knew what he wanted, or didn't want. We were such proud parents, nodding in agreement with all who suggested that his speech was well in advance of what might be expected for his age. We accepted that he was obviously very clever and considered the universities he might attend and the probable cures for serious illnesses he would discover. Our child was soaking up his surroundings and everything he encountered. He was a human sponge.

And that's where the difficulties started. From my uttering of 'ah for fuck's sake' after a box of eggs hit the floor to the many delightful phrases used in the older children's favourite television programme, *Father Ted*, his ability to articulate himself in colourful language grew. Almost worse than the language itself was his ability to use it in context. As his vocabulary grew, so did my nervousness about social situations. And so, once again, it came to pass that my fears were realised. I took my blonde-haired, green-eyed, angelic-looking cherub, who was feeling poorly, to see our GP. Our GP is great. He's warm, friendly and wonderful with kids. As he gently tried to have a look in my little boy's ear, the then two-year-old pulled away quickly and told the doctor that he was 'a big eejit'. Embarrassed, I hoped he hadn't been heard, but for good measure the two-year-old decided to repeat the compliment so that my GP was left in no doubt. Although my doctor laughed it off and didn't seem in the slightest bit fazed, I was absolutely mortified. I apologised over and over, mumbled an explanation about *Father Ted* fanatics living in my house and willed my toddler son not to treat my doctor to any more of his phraseology. I feared, leaving the surgery, that my son might drop something and respond in a similar manner to his less than perfect mother. I feared an old lady or gentleman might engage in conversation with my angelic-looking son and be treated to a Fr-Jack-like outburst, or worse still the theme tune to *The Wonder Pets* with the new words he had assigned to it. The fear was real. It was time to tackle it.

Breaking the Habit

Difficult as it may be to resist, don't laugh. Laughing at something that your toddler has said will just encourage them to repeat it. They might not understand that the word or phrase is offensive or unkind, but they will understand if it makes everyone laugh.

Ignoring the words or comments is worth a try. Sometime this will work; sometimes it won't. If it doesn't, offering an alternative word or phrase can help. Daft as you might feel, saying something like 'Oh dear' in an exaggerated tone when you drop something, staged or otherwise, can result in your little mimic copying you.

And be mindful of what they see and hear. You might think that things are going over their heads but toddlers absorb everything, including what you really think of your in-laws.

Tantrums

Toddler tantrums are infamous: that moment of ultimate meltdown when nothing is bringing them back from where they are. They're frustrated, they're overwhelmed, they're cross and they're going to let you know all about it. What's more, toddlers don't care where they are. Whether you're at home, visiting friends or relatives, or in the frozen food aisle of the supermarket, nowhere is out of bounds – and toddlers don't really care for your embarrassment.

No parent escapes the toddler/threenager stage of tantrums. It's a natural part of their development as your child tries to assert some independence and cope with lacking the vocabulary to adequately express their feelings and wants. It can be draining though, especially if it's the third tantrum of the day, or you're in a public place, limited by your surroundings. There are a few things that you can do, however, to minimise the frequency and fallout.

Prevention Is Better than Cure

- There are certain things likely to increase the risk of tantrums and these include tiredness and hunger. Don't be tempted to take your child grocery shopping if either of these are the case.
- Don't prolong a stay somewhere, squeezing in just one more thing and taking your child past their limit. When running errands, prioritise what needs to be done and if all is going well then decide if fitting something else in is truly an option.

- Avoid triggers. Stay away from the sweet and toy aisles, etc. in the shops if possible. At home, keep things that your child is not allowed to have out of sight and out of reach.
- Pick your battles. Some things matter, some things don't. Let your toddler have a little bit of say and control in the less important things as they struggle to assert their independence.
- Praise the good behaviour. If your child is happily strolling along beside you in the supermarket or on the school run, tell them how good they are. If they sit or play quietly while you try to coax a baby sibling to sleep, tell them how great they are.
- Distract, distract, distract. If you see that a tantrum is about to erupt, try to distract your child with a job to do, something to focus on (the little birdie over there) or a chat about plans for later that day.

Sometimes, of course, in spite of your best efforts, the tantrum will happen anyway. Public tantrums can feel difficult to manage, particularly if you sense that all eyes are on you. Chances are, however, that any parents looking your way are either feeling sympathy for you or relief that it's not their child this time.

My daughter managed a spectacular tantrum in the middle of the supermarket just two weeks before her brother was born. She was almost three and very tall for her age, so she looked older. With my enormous bump I found it impossible to lift her from her assumed position on the floor and no amount of pleading could coax her up from it. I felt that everyone was looking at me, and had I not believed that a crane would have been required to get me up again, I would have joined her quite happily complete with arms and legs flailing, such was my own frustration. On this occasion, I had to let that tantrum run its course because moving her was not an option. So I returned home after, with my face as tear-stained as my little girl's. Knowing how to react to the tantrum depends as much on the cause of it as on the individual child. I had one toddler whose tantrums always abated once the obligatory older lady sympathised with him, while another started the process all over again once the tantrum was acknowledged by an outsider at all. Some children just need to vocalise their frustrations and then all is forgotten about. Some need soothing and reassurance. As their parent you know best, so don't be dissuaded from the appropriate reaction by often well-intended but ill-advised friends, family and passers-by.

POTTY TRAINING

One of the most anticipated milestones of the toddler/threenager years is the leaving behind of nappies. The not so nice part is the road that has to be travelled to get there. Age alone is not enough to indicate when a child might be ready to potty train, but the majority of children will toilet train at around two or three years of age. As with every situation, there will always be some who will do it sooner and some who do it later. The important thing is to do it when you feel that your child is ready and not because of external pressures.

Some indications that your child may be ready can include:

• An awareness that they are pooing or weeing
• An ability to indicate to you that they need to poo
• A few hours passing with a dry/clean nappy
• An interest in others using the toilet
• A desire to have big boy/big girl pants
• Regular bowel habits
• An ability to follow basic instructions

Once you have decided to give it a go, be warned – you'll need the patience of a saint and shares in a kitchen roll company. Potty training is a wee and poo fest that the whole family can get involved in, so don't let anyone off the hook. Everyone can do their bit, including older siblings, and the more encouragement the potty-training child gets, the more likely they are to have success.

It's been said that girls are often ready to potty train at a younger age than boys. Personally I haven't found that to be the case. As luck would have it, most of my children have potty trained at a similar age, give or take a few weeks, although one child wasn't ready at the first time of trying so we took a break and revisited three weeks later to complete success. I have found that by three or four days into the process you will know if your child is truly ready. If, after that amount of time, your child is having more potty misses than potty success it may be worth postponing and trying again a few weeks later. There is no need to worry that all your hard work will go to waste. It won't, as your child will have more of an idea about what they are trying achieve the second or third time around.

A child who is ready will show signs of progression. A child who is not won't and the whole situation will prove incredibly stressful and prolonged for both you and your little one. Taking it step-by-step and day-by-day has proven, for me anyway, to be the quickest route to potty-training success.

Painless Potty Training

1. Potty training will need your full attention, so when choosing a time to begin make sure it's a time when you can be at home a little bit more. You may need to take a few days off work and stay at home as much as possible in the beginning. If you have school or after-school activity collections to do, it can make things more difficult so possibly choose a weekend or a school holiday period to begin. Failing that, see if you can rope someone in to help with pick-ups. Plan in advance and discourage visitors if at all possible. Potty training is a new skill and, like all new skills, requires a lot focus and concentration. Distractions are not great for your little one at this time.

2. Try to involve your child in the choosing of their own potty. Where possible go along with their choice. A particular colour or preschool character is likely to hold a lot more attraction for your potty-training child than a potty which appears super practical to you but is less eye-catching for them. Involve them also in the purchase of their big boy/big girl pants. Again character and colour is likely to be the big draw here. All the while remind your child of how grown up they're becoming and how now that they have a potty and big boy/big girl pants, they won't need to wear nappies any more.

3. On the first day of training, allow your child to go without either a nappy or pants. They will be reminded of the absence of the nappy if they're wearing nothing. The presence of pants however, can confuse them and make them forget that the nappy is missing.

   Make sure the potty is always visible and offer drinks frequently. The idea on the first day is to 'catch' a wee in the potty by chance. Plenty of fluids will not only increase the opportunities for you to do this, but will also make sure that your little one doesn't hold on. If you can bear it, it's worth putting the potty in front of the TV and turning on their favourite programme so that they can sit on the potty as they watch. The appeal of the potty is often lost after sitting on it for a couple of minutes, so the distraction can prove a big help.

   Waiting for your child to wee can take longer than you might originally have anticipated. This is because the security of the nappy is gone and they can feel reluctant to 'let go'.

4. When your child finally produces something, if you managed to keep them sitting there for a period it will most likely have been just by chance. They may not even realise that they have gone until they stand up. This is when it's time to make an enormous fuss. Hugs, praise, everything – the full shebang. Involve any other family members who are around in the praise-giving. Call them down the stairs to admire the contents and go full throttle on the applause. Your little one now has an idea of what they're supposed to do in the potty.

5. Prepare to shadow your child everywhere, literally everywhere. Small children get pretty bored with the whole potty thing very quickly and are quite likely to run off and pee somewhere else. (One of mine had a tendency to disappear and poo in the corner of our dining room. The poo remained undiscovered until someone went into the room and encountered the 'aroma').

   Move the potty from room to room as your child moves about the house. If there are older siblings, ask them to help with the shadowing. If your child starts to wee while they're not on the potty, just quickly lift them up and place them on it. Anything in there is better than nothing, and remind them that all wees should be done in the potty.

6. Throughout the day, keep saying to your child, 'Where do we do wees and poos? … In the potty.' You might feel like a broken record but the constant reminders are a must. All success throughout the day should be heavily praised and misses met with a gentle reminder that wees and poos are done in the potty.

7. When it's time for bed, don't revert to the usual style nappy, but instead place your child in a pull-up type. Don't refer to the pull-up as a nappy but merely as a different type of big boy/big girl pants. No one is expecting this to be dry in the morning, but it's good to make the distinction between this and a nappy. It continues the idea that your child is now a big boy/big girl and it prepares the way for pulling up and down pants which will be introduced over the coming days.

8. Begin day two in much the same way as day one. Remove the pull-up as soon as your child wakes. Once again the child shouldn't wear a nappy or pants. Keep the potty close at hand and always in your child's line of vision. Day two can sometimes be met with more resistance as the novelty begins to wear off. Praise, gentle insistence and bribery can help.

   On day two your child might know that they have produced a wee and may well jump up to show you (or not, which is no problem either). Again shadowing is really important so as not to miss an opportunity.

9. Later on, in day two (or day three if you feel your child is not ready) introduce the big boy/big girl pants. You can be pretty much guaranteed that an accident will happen early on but that's ok because the wet sensation will remind your little one of what happens if they don't make it to the potty on time. Make sure someone is on hand at all times to help your child to pull up and down their pants throughout the day and any success here should again be met with a huge fuss.

   If your child manages to wee or poo in the potty after having pulled down their pants there is a good chance that your child recognised the sensation of needing to wee and deliberately used the potty. They may, on several occasions during the day however, tell you that they need to wee and then produce nothing. This is very normal and typical as they become familiar with the feeling of needing to go.

10. Day three should continue in a similar fashion to the previous day, with hopefully a little more success. It's quite likely, however, that you may have encountered some resistance to pooing in the potty. This is a difficult one to balance. It's important to make sure that your little one doesn't become constipated or holds on to their poo. If your child indicates that they need to poo, remove their pants again so that they can easily get to the potty at the very last minute. Again consider allowing your child to watch a favourite programme and encourage them to sit on the potty while they do. Hopefully they'll get so caught up in what they're watching that they will produce. If your child is reluctant, however, to sit on the potty for any period of time, offering some additional bribery, such as a little treat, may help.

Often just managing to poo that first or second time in the potty is all that is required to ensure that your child is comfortable going in the future. It may be worth leaving the child without pants again for a while to see if this helps. If your little one becomes very distressed and still refuses to go, put a pull-up style nappy on them (still referring to them as big boy or girl pants). Continue to encourage them to poo in the potty but don't worry if they go in the pull-up nappy instead. Pooing in the potty always takes a little longer to master and, like wees, it may be necessary to 'catch' a poo that first time.

By day four you should have real idea as to how your child is getting on. If they're having less than a 50–60 per cent success rate they're probably not quite ready yet and you might be better off just leaving it for a few more weeks (even just three weeks can make an enormous difference). Don't worry that all your hard work will be wasted, it won't. Starting again a few weeks later should be easier, as your child will know what you and they are aiming for. Progress can often be much faster then.

11. As the days pass you may decide to brave an outing with your potty-training child. Before you leave the house, encourage your child to use the potty and place a pull-up on them (though continue to refer to the pull-ups as big boy/big girl pants). Remind them to tell you if they need to do a wee or poo and make sure that you know where the toilets are once you arrive.

    You may need to constantly ask your child while you're out if they need to go, as the new environment, without a potty in their line of vision, can lead to them forgetting. The pull-up will help, however, if they do. If your child does say that they need to go, get ready to run fast. You won't get much warning in the early days between their saying and their doing.

12. If things are going well, keep an eye on the night-time pull-ups. Some children day and night train at the same time. If you're one of the lucky parents whose child appears to be dry at night also, remove the pull-up after about a week into potty training.

    Remember to make sure your little one goes to the toilet before bed and don't offer drinks too late in the evening. If your child, however, is not dry in the morning when they wake, don't worry; one step at a time. Night-time dryness can be tackled later. Hormones play a part in night-time dryness so it's not something that can or should be forced.

Praise, praise and more praise is the order of the day when it comes to potty training. Encouragement, constant reminders and reaffirmations that the child is a big boy or girl now are essential. Once the child has mastered the idea, accidents become less and less and you'll get more warning before action as time passes.

When progressing to the toilet from the potty, a toilet seat can help your child to feel secure and less nervous, as can a step to support their feet. The transition can take from a few days to a few weeks. Don't rush things, stay calm and keep things positive. Your child may well spend the first few times on the toilet with their arms tightly around your neck so that they don't 'fall down the hole', but don't worry, the panic won't last.

Montessori and Preschool

Soon after your toddler/threenager is potty trained, you may find that they are eligible to attend Montessori or preschool. Once an optional extra, it now appears to be the general norm for parents to avail of this extra year or two of education in preparation for 'big school'.

Many children are delighted to start Montessori, embracing the fact that they are big boys and girls, with teachers, friends and busy work to do. Others are terrified and horrified at the prospect of being separated from their parents or usual minder. As in so many aspects of life, we've had all types here. Some have loved the structure and the environment so much so that they've opted to attend Montessori on their birthday, just so they could wear the birthday crown and have their friends and teacher sing the birthday song. Some have seen fellow Montessori attendees and indeed their teachers as an audience for their artistic displays. By this I mean child number three who won an award for the most fantastic stories every day. One of these included a story where his dad had apparently told him that 'he wouldn't let him sleep in his bed, even if he was growing on his ass'. The observant among you may have recognised that quote from the children's movie *Home Alone*, when Kevin's big brother afforded him such consideration. What was it I mentioned earlier about being mindful of what they see and hear ...? Others have experienced mysterious and suspicious illnesses day on day that have allegedly rendered them unfit for school. No one has actually hated it, but some are just less bothered than others.

For parents, it's often viewed as the first step on the path to growing up. The first steps towards independence. I wouldn't equate it with the first day at primary school, but the first day at preschool is a momentous occasion nonetheless. Preschool and Montessori are often a first opportunity for a child to make friends in your absence. It's a new environment where your child can learn to negotiate situations with other children, learning respect and consideration of others' needs along the way. In addition to many daily activities, children even master some of the practical skills necessary ahead of starting primary school, such as using the toilet, packing their bags and managing their lunchboxes and beakers. And dare I say it, for the parents at home it's a few hours toddler/threenager free.

Preparation

Preparing your child for Montessori in advance of their first day is important. Because of the age of the child involved, however, it can be hard to adequately explain what to expect, but many preschools and Montessori schools are very happy to allow children to drop in and explore their forthcoming new surroundings in advance of D-day. In the days leading up to beginning preschool, chat positively with your child about the exciting start that's coming up. Take them to buy a new school bag and maybe even a new top with their favourite character on it to wear on the first day. For the first few days, send your child to preschool for a shorter amount of time than will be their norm. Let them gradually adjust to their new routine and lengthen their day bit by bit.

Montessori and preschool are not school, though they are wonderful preparations for it. As a parent, it's important not to become too bogged down in upset or fretfulness about whether or not your child is ready. This is not a school setting. This is a happy, learning and creative environment. The children who attend at any one time can range from two-and-a-half to six years of age, so comparing children at the drop-off or pick-up is particularly pointless. Developmentally, the children can be at very different stages.

Check in with your child's preschool/Montessori teacher if you're worried about how your child is managing when you're not there. They can give you some insight into how things are really going and possibly put your mind at ease.

***

The toddler and threenager years generally come to an end with your barely noticing. The transition from headless-chicken-like toddler to threenager sees a more opinionated and assertive child take over. The battles are different, the attitude more forceful and the newly acquired language and negotiation skills more articulate. The way in which they view the world, however, remains just as fantastic.

But as four candles adorn the birthday cake, you'll realise that somewhere along the way the strops have become less frequent, the battles less fraught and an almost reasonable and sometimes even rational human being has assumed your little one's place.

A seamless change has happened and your threenager has now become a 'proper' little boy or little girl. Still full of fun, still full of laughter and still full of mischief, but hopefully with the tiniest bit more sense and understanding.

6

Time for Another?

Mother Nature is great. She has a way of painting things in the most wonderful light in your head and wiping certain things temporarily from your memory. Although parenthood may not have been exactly as you expected and sleep deprivation more tortuous than you anticipated; although childbirth may have been more excruciating than you imagined and babies more time-consuming than you appreciated; although breastfeeding may have meant that your once fashionable self is now confined to a wardrobe of accessible separates, and your pale trousers all have yellow-tinged poo marks on them that just refuse to come out in the wash; and although it's all been a rollercoaster and a half and you hadn't the strongest of stomachs to begin with, one day you may well find that you'd like to add to your numbers.

And when that day happens, you will remember all of the blissful things about pregnancy and childbirth and having a new baby, and those happy, blissful thoughts will stay to the front of your mind always and forever – until you pee on that stick and once again see those familiar two lines. And then panic will set in when you remember that you have a squeeze a baby out again.

But ahead of that panic there are many things to consider, assuming that a few drinks on a Friday night don't negate your need to plan (ahem, hello child number six). What suits one person might not suit another and our individual expectations from life can vary hugely. All that being said, there are a few things worth factoring in when deciding if the time is right to add to your numbers, or indeed whether or not to take the plunge into outnumbered-dom and beyond.

THE PERFECT AGE GAP

There is no such thing as the perfect age gap, there are just different age gaps, all with their own benefits and challenges. Some people are keen to keep the gap small in the hope of children growing up together as friends. Others prefer the idea of a bigger age gap, perhaps not wanting to add to their numbers until their older child is at school.

One factor to bear in mind is that the age gap between siblings is not always within our control. For those lucky enough to have experienced no difficulty with the conception of their first (or subsequent children), it's easy to fall into the belief that the gap between your children is largely down to your choice. Life, unfortunately, doesn't always play out like that.

I've been very lucky in my life not to have experienced any major fertility difficulties. Many people comment on the spacing of my children as if it was good planning on my part. Most of the children have a two or two-and-a-half year age gap between them. There is, however, almost three years between my first two children. Not a significant age gap by any stretch of the imagination, but a bigger one than I had hoped or planned for.

My second pregnancy ended in miscarriage shortly after the three-month mark. It was a difficult recovery, both emotionally and physically. In my grief, all I wanted was to be pregnant again. It took almost a year before I was. Age was not a factor; I was in my mid-twenties. The previous two pregnancies, incredibly, had seen me fall pregnant the first month of trying. This was a very new experience for me.

As turned out, the three-year gap worked out well. My daughter and eldest son were, and still are, very close – but it wasn't the gap that I had aimed for. Best-laid plans had to take a back seat to nature's crueller plans.

In spite of the fairly consistent age gaps between the children, having a larger family means that I also have to juggle the larger age gaps and age span that exist between the older and younger members of the family. It can be a challenge, but it has its upsides too and it's the case for anyone brave enough to go beyond two children.

The Pros of a Smaller Age Gap

- You have readymade playmates with children at a similar stage of life.
- You're still in that baby/toddler stage so the adjustment back to coping with a new baby is not as difficult.
- As they grow they may have similar friends and you may be able to involve them in similar activities.
- It can make childcare choices easier.

And the Cons …

- Resting during pregnancy is unlikely to be an option with a very small child to look after.
- When baby arrives, it can be exhausting dealing with the needs of a baby and a toddler at the same time.
- You may have the additional expense of having to double up – an additional cot, a similar car seat, a double buggy, even two sets of the same toys to avoid arguments.
- Two in nappies at the same time – enough said.

The Pros of a Larger Age Gap

- You have the opportunity to take care of yourself a little better during pregnancy with a less demanding older child.
- Your body has had a chance to recover between pregnancies.
- An older sibling can understand what's going on and can better appreciate the needs of a baby and some of the restrictions.
- The older child may be able to help with simple tasks and help occupy baby for you too.

- You will have the opportunity to give your younger child some one-on-one time while your older child is at school.
- The baby equipment is freed up.

And the Cons ...

- Returning to the baby stage can involve an adjustment, particularly if you've left the sleepless nights and nappies behind and your current youngest has assumed a certain level of independence with care.
- Siblings are less likely to be playmates.
- A large gap means that they're unlikely to have similar interests as they're at very different stages of childhood.
- Finding a childcare solution that can work around a school-attending child and a baby can be slightly more complicated.
- The logistics can be difficult to manage when it comes to trying to fit baby's routine around school runs and after-school activities.
- Any comfortable work–life balance you may have established may need to be reviewed to work around the very different needs of the age groups involved.

Of course things can be thrown further askew if you choose to have a third child or more. At that stage, there is the age gap to consider between eldest and youngest as well as between each individual child. It can be a bit of a minefield, and definitely for me is one of the most challenging aspects of having a larger family. Meeting the needs of all the age groups at any given time, navigating the logistical nightmare that ensues, and finding an activity that will suit and occupy everyone can be near impossible. Compromise is the only solution.

As life gets in the way of our own ideals, that 'perfect' age gap may not materialise for many different reasons. And while we all want our children to be close and to be friends, an age gap at either end of the spectrum is unlikely to be the single determining factor. Personalities have a significant role to play and, as any parent of more than one child knows, even with the same ingredients very different results can be produced.

FINANCIAL CONSIDERATIONS

Having children is expensive and the more you have, it stands to reason, the more expensive it gets. The good news is that for second and subsequent children you probably already have a lot of the baby equipment, such as a car seat, pram and cot (although you will need a new cot and/or Moses basket mattress for each new baby). You'll probably also have a lot of the bedding, a playmat and early baby toys and gadgets. If you have the same gender, you'll probably even have the clothes.

And there are ways to work around some of the extras that you might need. If the gap between your babies is small, it's worth checking with a friend or relative if they have a double buggy that you can borrow. You may only need the double buggy for a relatively short period of time before you can revert to your own single one, so it might not be worth the expense of buying one anyway. If an additional cot is needed, again it's worth asking if anyone has one to spare, although you still can't avoid the cost of a new mattress. This is a safety issue and linked with reducing the risk of SIDS (Sudden Infant Death Syndrome).

Adorable little babies, however, grow into equally adorable but much more financially demanding children. Children grow like weeds, and clothes and shoes can have a limited lifespan. When school comes onto the horizon, the cost of school books, uniforms, stationery, voluntary contributions, school trips and endless donations towards endless causes can really mount up. After-school activities and all the equipment that goes hand-in-hand with them can be surprisingly expensive, and then there are the many camps that may be necessary to cover some of the school holidays if you work outside the home. Suitable-sized cars (or not-so-fashionable minibuses) may be required to accommodate car seats and transport your growing brood. Family outings, holidays and treats all become much more expensive as your numbers grow.

Without a money tree in the back garden, the many costs coming down the line can be enough to put you off completely and without a crystal ball it's difficult to know what any of our financial positions might be by the time these expenses come knocking. While a sense of realism is important, so too is the necessity to appreciate what truly matters to you as a person. The ideals you hold for your family will not necessarily be the same as the ideals your own friends or family hold, and that's perfectly fine, but you may need to remind yourself of that fact. Expenses can be prioritised depending on this.

Some of the many costs can be reduced through obvious means – the passing on of school books, uniforms and clothes; holidaying mostly at home; choosing family outings wisely, and bringing along a packed lunch for days out. This mum of many is also eternally grateful for the progressive sibling discounts offered by a variety of after-school activities.

And then there's the age-old question of affording college. It's very important to me that my children can realise their potential. In due course I would like to think that we can support them in whatever road they take and help them to avail of whatever further studies they choose. Will having a part-time job to help cover the expense really harm them? I don't think so. It certainly didn't harm me and, if anything, it will probably teach them an important lesson about the value of money.

THE CHILDCARE CONUNDRUM

Although it may seem as if it could come under the heading of costs, the subject of childcare is more complicated in its consideration. The financial aspect is probably already substantial, and potentially amounts to a second mortgage for many, but a practical element also needs attention. Some childminders and childcare facilities offer a discount for siblings. Others charge per individual child. It's easy to see with your existing childcare arrangement if the financial demands are manageable.

For me, the work-sharing pattern that I adopted following the birth of my first child has meant that I have never had more than two children in childcare at any one time. Luck, some might think. An essential, is the reality. With reduced working hours naturally comes reduced pay. My work-sharing pattern, of mornings only, means that only my youngest children are in childcare, while my eldest are at school. The school holidays and the number of children means that I have often needed to avail of parental leave over the summer holidays. I have yet to meet a childminder brave enough, or crazy enough, to take on all seven and, truth be told, if such a person did exist they would probably charge more than I earn.

While my needs may have been brought about because of a larger than typical family, other much more usual situations can also create problematic childcare scenarios. Shift work, children requiring different pick-ups, or even family-based childcare with a relative who just can't manage to take care of any more children may call your family-adding plans into question. Staying at home might be something that you find you'll need to consider, but it is not always an option. The childcare conundrum is something that will need real consideration sooner rather than later, as the need for childcare is not as far down the road after baby's birth as other costs and issues. It can be a make-or-break issue when it comes to family planning.

THE CURRENT DEMANDS

More kids means more work – more laundry, more tears, more tantrums, more cooking, more cleaning, more refereeing, more sleepless nights and in due course more homework. It also, of course, means more love too. The demands of parenthood as children get older, and the workload, don't necessarily lessen, they just evolve, and hopefully by a later stage you're managing that workload on a full night's sleep.

I have to be honest, I've never really subscribed to the notion that two is twice the work of one, that three is three times, or even that seven is seven times the work. With your first-born child, you are their sole playmate, comforter, protector and fixer of all things. You are the person with whom they chat about *Peppa Pig*, their favourite toy, what's going on at school and what's troubling them. As your first child, they are your guinea pig. They give you your first taste of parenthood and first insights into parenting and its all-consuming nature. With second and subsequent children, you have an idea of what's involved, and that familiarity means that you tend to be more relaxed. You also have a right-hand woman or man in the shape of your eldest or older children. Their new role as big brother or big sister will, in all likelihood, see them happy to assume the position of chief playmate. Your youngest child will know that their older sibling can help to reach that dropped soother or toy they need, and is just as good as mum and dad at peek-a-boo. The fact that their sibling seems to enjoy playing with toys more than mum and dad is a bonus. All this help may mean that you even get a chance to finish your coffee while it's hot.

A new family dynamic, however, will always be created by the arrival of another child. There will be more demands and restrictions on your time and this can actually be more apparent if you have older children at school. My younger children have to fit in around the lives of their older siblings. There's no way around it. If I need to collect a child from school and one of my younger children is tired, they still have to come with me. Naptimes must work around the older children's needs. It feels cruel sometimes, particularly when I reflect on how different things were for the older children as babies and toddlers, but it's a necessity of our family dynamic.

When the evening comes around and I've run around after a toddler all day, endured homework battles, made dinners, cleaned up, built a tent out the back for the wannabe cowboys and Indians, and I'm ready to collapse onto the couch, I find myself surrounded by my older children, who obviously go to bed later than their younger counterparts. Some evenings I need to pop out to collect an older child from the cinema or a friend's house, or bring another to sports training or music practice.

When I had toddlers and small children alone, the evening was mine from seven o'clock, give or take ten or twenty trips up and down the stairs to settle the restless baby. Now with a broader age span, the demands of the day are more and go on longer. Some of this undoubtedly is down to the number of children, but much of it is related to the age gap between the eldest and youngest. Three children in a family with an age spread similar to the gap between my eldest and youngest might not create the same amount of laundry, but would probably result in a similarly long day.

On top of parenting, many of us have outside responsibilities, including work, outside interests/hobbies and extended family commitments. As individual as our unique families are, so too are our responsibilities. The current trend towards having children later in life sees many people now deemed as 'the sandwich generation', caught between caring for their children and caring for elderly parents.

Juggling the many demands and asks is no mean feat. Maintaining a balance is difficult. When it comes down to it, only you and your partner know if another child might upset the equilibrium beyond manageability. None of us are truly in the exact same position, even those with whom we appear to have so much in common, so there is no point in comparing.

As family and other commitments vary, so too do levels of support. Some people have family living close by, willing and able to help out in any way they can. Others live a distance away, or have no one in a position to even lend a hand when a child is ill. Support, or lack thereof, can make all the difference.

And then there are those who just seem to manage and cope differently and are affected differently by varied demands and asks. There is no obvious reason why, it's just how they are. The world would be a very boring place if we were all the same, and we're very obviously not. How much we can each manage is as individual as we are.

THE AGE-OLD QUESTION

Thirty is the new twenty, forty is the new thirty – and so it goes. Age is just a number it's alleged, and while that might be true in many instances, nature unfortunately doesn't always concur. As we age our fertility declines, in spite of a range of celebrities apparently begging to differ. The harsh reality, however, is that getting older makes it more difficult to become pregnant and to maintain a pregnancy.

Many women are choosing to start their families later in life, while for others motherhood comes at a later stage for a variety of different reasons. While this later start is pretty much the norm these days, it does means that our age has to be taken into account, sometimes sooner than we'd like – especially when it comes to factoring in the possibility of another child.

For many people, forty seems to be a subconscious cut-off point, as if our fertility drops off the cliff, and the risks associated with pregnancy at a later age suddenly increase just one day past a fortieth birthday. Our fertility, however, unfortunately begins to decline several years before that. While every woman is, of course, different and fertility levels can appear to vary dramatically from woman to woman, it would be naive to ignore the potential significance of your age when it comes to making plans.

Of course it's not just in terms of fertility that age needs to be considered. There's also the fact that you will also be older at every stage of parenthood. How much of an issue that is though depends on you. I've heard people say that they felt much more tired on a third or fourth child and blamed their tiredness on their age. I am much more tired on my seventh child. I can categorically tell you that it is not because of my age. Yes I am older now than I was when I had my first. I'm also older now than I was when I had my sixth, such are the laws of time. I am more tired now because there are seven children to contend with and having seven children involves a lot of work, and not so much sleep.

In contrast, however, I feel that I have more energy now than when I had my first child; it's just that I have to preserve it for parenting, rather than clubbing. Parenthood is a marathon, not a sprint. All of the years of training that have been put in means that I am used to accomplishing all number and manner of things at once, in spite of limited sleeping opportunities or even sitting-down opportunities. All of those years of training have built up a strength and resilience that the first-time much younger mum me could only dream of. That energy, of course, may just be a manifestation of sleep-deprived delirium. To be honest, it's so long since I've slept I can't be 100 per cent sure, but whatever it is I'm full of it. As for the rest of it, if you're in good health then that 'age is only a number' claim rings true. Yes, you will be older again when your child is in school and a teenager, but they'll keep you young at heart and you'll have even more life experience and insights to share with them.

So, once you have decided that you're ready to add to your numbers, and once you've taken the plunge and there's a new baby on board, it's time to start getting ready for the new family dynamic that awaits.

PREPARING THE OLDER CHILDREN

I have always loved telling my children that a new baby was on the way and found it very hard to keep it a secret until I felt the time was right. That time differed depending on the age of the child I was telling. On the most recent pregnancies, I told my daughter straight away. In saying that, she was older and therefore had a better concept of time and, unfortunately, an understanding that there was always a chance that the pregnancy wouldn't go as I hoped.

My other children were kept in the dark a little longer. Patience isn't a virtue that many children are blessed with, and the constant questions about 'how many more days', never mind months, didn't appeal. To be honest, I was also a little nervous about breaking exciting news to them that I might later have to change. I found it impossible to go through future pregnancies unaffected by previous experiences.

How long you can get away without telling your children depends on many things. One is how astute they are. My eldest child was immediately suspicious when she spotted the rekindling of the relationship between my head and the toilet bowl. 'I think Mum has a baby in her tummy' she told her dad when she was just four years of age, just in case he hadn't realised.

My third child was always on the lookout and he assumed it was a given that a new baby would arrive after a certain amount of time. One day, shortly after baby number six arrived, I went out for a walk with all of the children. We met an elderly lady, who stopped to admire the baby and asked if all of the children were mine. As I confirmed that they were indeed, child three, my shy guy, perked up and told her, 'If you come back in two years, we'll have another baby. Mum gets a new one every two years.' I never realised that he had been paying attention, or the conclusions he had drawn.

Waiting to tell a younger child can make a lot of sense, because of their lack of time comprehension. You can generally get away that little bit longer without them noticing your growing belly. Assuming that the pregnancy progresses without any complications that involve a hospital stay, the timing can be very much within your control. The only danger in leaving it too long to tell them is that either somebody in the know slips up and mentions it in front of them, or an individual less oblivious to your disappearing waist and growing abdomen congratulates you in their presence.

The advantage of telling a slightly older child, when you feel ready to do so, is that you can explain why you can't pick the couch up to look for their missing *Star Wars* figure and why they really shouldn't use your bed as a trampoline at 6 a.m. on a Saturday morning while you're still in it. They can also understand why you're too tired to take them to the playground that day and they may even feel inclined to help you around the house a little bit – the operative word being 'may'. I have to stress that this is far from a given.

How each child handles the news will depend very much on the individual child. Some will be immediately delighted at the prospect – a real-life walking, talking, pooping doll to play with, in their eyes someone on whom they can impart their infinite wisdom. Other children will be horrified at the idea of sharing their parents for the first time, or again, and some will just be much more concerned about what's for dinner.

Getting Them Ready

- Chat about the new arrival in a really positive tone. Tell your older child what a fantastic big brother/sister they will be to the new baby and how much the baby is going to love them.
- Give them the chance to ask questions and don't brush off any concerns they may have, such as not being your baby anymore.

- Don't underestimate the impact on an older child too. Yes they can understand that they're getting a new sibling, but they possibly can also understand the amount of attention that a baby needs, and they may worry about being displaced. This was surprisingly true for me when it came to having my fifth child. Old hands at hearing baby news, I expected the children to embrace it completely and most did. My daughter, however, was quite worried about what would happen if the baby was a girl. She had had eight years of being the only daughter and the only granddaughter. She needed reassurance that nothing would change and that she would always be our baby girl, no matter who came along or how old she was.
- If you're having a hospital birth, closer to the time explain that you will/may be there for a few days. It's best to have them prepared for your leave of absence.
- Involve your child/children in preparing for baby's arrival. Let them help you to choose babygros, bibs and other baby essentials you are purchasing. When you're freshening up baby items in the wash show them to your other child or children. They'll be especially fascinated if it's something they wore themselves as babies.

Buying a gift for your older children from the new baby is a great idea. It helps to get them off on the right foot. If your child is old enough to take the call, maybe let them be first to receive the news of baby's arrival, and, if the news wasn't previously known, to discover whether they have a brother or a sister.

A new sibling's arrival is just the first part. All will change at home as a new person comes to join the party. This isn't a bad thing of course, but there can be an adjustment required as everyone in the house assumes a new role, possibly with new responsibilities and certainly new expectations.

THE NEW DYNAMIC

You've arrived home, exhausted, probably sore, but very much in love with this new, tiny, little person whom you've managed to create. Your toddler is waiting, either completely unforgivingly or with overwhelming excitement, and your older children are ready for life to return to normal – baby is out now after all.

Welcome to parenthood the second, third or more times around. Yes, you and baby still need to get to know each other. Yes, you still need time to establish breastfeeding and recover from childbirth. And yes, you still need some well-earned rest, but, this time around, sleeping when baby sleeps is not an option because there are other little people, with boundless energy, who unfortunately don't require the same level of napping. Then there's fact that you've probably been missing in action for a few days, so there's a lot of catching up for you to do and things for you to sort out that you couldn't do over the last few days because you were off having a baby.

All sounds delightful, but the big advantage you have this time is experience. You'll know that some things can't be hurried, but you'll be a dab hand at nappy-changing, bathing and burping, and all the other things that had to be learned the first time around. The part that you have to learn now is how to re-juggle everything.

When all settles down, the initial excitement has passed, and you're left more or less to your own devices, to continue with your family in its new form, it can be a shock to the system. Taking care of a new baby in addition to a toddler and/or school runs, and the challenges that go with having children of different ages, is not easy. The sometimes 'go with the flow' needs of a new baby don't fit so neatly into the more structured routine of a toddler or schoolchild.

You will need eyes in the back of your head, an infinite amount of patience and an ability to accept the limitations and the confines involved with meeting the needs of your younger and older child/ children, but it will all come good, eventually. In the interim, here are a few things to bear in mind:

- Newborns sleep a lot, an awful lot. If your older child is finding the adjustment difficult and is still at home with you during the day, baby's naptime is the perfect time for you to spend some quality time with them – reading a book, playing a game or just having a cuddle.

- Try to involve your older child in your baby's care. It will help them to feel included and to feel better about their role as the big brother or sister. Lots of compliments along the way should mean your little one will happily oblige. It can be something as simple as getting a nappy or baby vest for you, to a more fun activity like helping with bathtime.

- Be aware that the help is likely to continue in your absence. Monkey see, monkey do applies even when you would prefer it didn't. Baby number six needed a lot of protection from child number five, who at breakneck speed would run to his little brother's side in the event of any tears or noise. On one occasion child five decided that his baby brother obviously wanted to go for a walk in his buggy – not my baby's buggy you understand, but rather child number five's toy buggy – and so he proceeded to drag baby six by the ankles out from his playmat with the plan of replacing teddy with real-life baby brother. You learn to run very fast when you have a baby and a toddler at the same time – if not to save your baby from being dropped by an older well-meaning toddler, then to prevent your baby being force-fed an orange ice pop at just a few weeks old by that same well-meaning toddler, because 'sharing is caring'.

- As baby gets older suggest that your older child plays peek-a-boo or some similar game that's likely to make your baby smile or laugh. Kids love to be the reason a baby laughs and having fun together really helps to strengthen and build on their relationship.

- Prioritising matters even more when you're bound by school or preschool collections. Baby's naps will not always fit around your timetable. Make sure you eat, make sure baby eats and accept the unavoidable. Sometimes baby will have to nap en route to collecting their older sibling. It's not ideal, but it's life. The luxury of working around baby's sleep time is often restricted to first babies only.

- On that note, don't beat yourself up about not being able to provide the exact same standard of care that you afforded your firstborn, that's just a privilege of being the eldest. You're still providing excellent care, it's just different.

- Try not to fall into the trap whereby your partner does everything with the older child and you are always with the baby. It's a very easy habit to fall into, but it could make your older child feel excluded in spite of your best efforts. If going places as a family is not yet an option, switch responsibilities wherever possible. Let your partner bathe baby while you do bathtime with your older child. Even if it's just sitting down watching TV together, let your partner hold baby while your older child sits on your lap or cuddles up to you. Anything which reminds your older child that they still have access to you whenever they want or need.
- Say yes to any offers of help. It's more important now that ever and help can come in so many different forms. The help that I appreciate more than any other has to be when somebody comes to visit and willingly agrees, or eventually relents (to be honest, desperation means I'm usually not that bothered which it is), to wait at my house with my younger children while I do the school run. The bliss and the freedom of being able to walk to school without dragging a reluctant superhero behind me, or chasing after him if the mood so takes him, while negotiating a toddler-laden buggy at the same time, is just indescribable. Help does indeed come in many forms when you're outnumbered.

Knowing that every stage is a passing phase means that motherhood, second and subsequent times around, doesn't necessarily provide the same shock to the system. Watching your family grow and relationships develop between your children can be a tonic for the soul, especially after a demanding and stress-filled day. In fact, it can be such a tonic that in spite of swearing on the labour ward that this is it – boy, girl, amphibian, whatever – there will absolutely, positively, most definitely, without a doubt, categorically, never, ever, ever be any more babies – yes in spite of these declarations of certainty – you may find yourself changing your mind yet again.

So how many is too many, and is there such a thing as a magic number? Does that 'done' feeling ever really happen, or does Mother Nature keep us clucky all the way to the menopause?

LARGER FAMILIES

For all manner of reasons, families are smaller now than they were in our parents' and grandparents' time. The new cultural norm means that anything over two or three children is considered a large family. I swore while giving birth to my second child that two was going to be my magic number. Not because I had an ideal of two in my head, but because his birth was particularly difficult. When he arrived, all gorgeous and perfect and surprisingly male (three sisters and one daughter later, I never envisaged having a son), I forgot the promise I had made to myself, very loudly, only moments earlier. 'He's fabulous', I told my husband. 'We should have lots of these.'

Child number two just slotted in. Calm from birth, it's quite fitting that he was the youngest of all his siblings to smile. His sister adored him. As he grew, he allowed her to lead the way and followed her instructions and games happily. The transition from one to two couldn't have been easier. In fact it was so easy that my husband suggested, when baby number two was just six months old, that maybe we should consider a third child.

While we didn't opt to have another quite so soon, baby number three did arrive just days before his big brother's second birthday. His pregnancy had been a worrying time as a scan had picked up a kidney issue that was unclear and an unstable lie and impressive birthweight saw the occurrence of my first C-section.

Child number three had a more difficult start in life. His immature lungs meant he spent his first few days in the Special Care Baby Unit. With his kidney condition still unclear, he was started immediately on prophylactic antibiotics. In complete contrast to his big brother, child number three did not just slot in. Endless and sometimes invasive tests and procedures saw frequent hospital stays, while his compromised immune system left him vulnerable to a serious infection which resulted in him spending a terrifying few days in intensive care. The children at home were uprooted and unsettled as their mum and dad juggled hospital visits and home life.

Baby number three was very unsettled and cried for significant periods of the day and night. A lot of this was caused by the discomfort he was in. As his parents it was difficult to see and hear our baby in pain, and at the same time to witness the constant disruption to our older children's lives. In fairness to them they never complained, but they were very small and it was hard for them to have so much uncertainty week-on-week.

Child number three, incidentally, is a strapping eleven-year-old now, whose kidney issues have been resolved, but his condition meant that he did not just slot in, with all returning to normal following his birth. In saying that, there was nothing we could do but we did naively underestimate the transition. As for children four, five, six and seven, they all arrived – thankfully healthy and well – and assumed their place in the family certainly, but each child created a new dynamic and a new normal. 'Slotting in' suggests that nothing changes. Every child, no matter how chilled, brings about a change.

And yet in spite of the endless changes, continuing challenges and the constant returning to sleepless nights, nappies and toddler tantrums, I felt driven to have more children. I have been assured that I will know when I'm done. Apparently there is a 'feeling'. I'm not completely convinced. I've come to the conclusion that the 'done' feeling probably only comes about if you get to where you need to be. If you have a certain number in your head, for example, that you don't want to veer from. If you have a personal family ideal you would like to replicate. Or, perhaps, if you feel driven to experience parenting both genders. If you don't have a definite idea of where you want to be then you'll probably choose to be done, rather than 'feeling' it.

I've heard it all and been asked it all. I have been asked if gender balance was my driving force. It's not. Had it been I would have stopped at two, when I had a much more socially acceptable 'gentleman's family'. Gender has always been irrelevant to me. I have been asked if religious beliefs were a factor. They're not either. And I have a TV, I know what causes it, and I understand how contraception works.

But I do hear lovely things too, and mostly when people stop me to comment it's to say something positive, something congratulatory even. I'm told lovely stories of happy childhoods growing up as part of a big family. I'm told how lucky they are to have each other and how lucky I am to have them. That much I know, and I'm eternally grateful.

But it's silly to pretend that it's all a bed of roses. I may be biased, but I think large families are great. They do, however, come with much more laundry, many more commitments, much less sleep, much more love and much more mayhem.

The Realities of a Big Family

Today's world is not designed for large families. Family rooms at hotels normally accommodate just two, or at a push maybe three, children. Family tickets for shows and theme parks often only allow for a smaller number of children and 'kids eat free' offers at restaurants never apply to a larger-sized family. Coupled with the fact that your car choices for transporting your troops are limited and siblings sharing a bedroom several times over are part of your family's reality, it doesn't take much reminding to flag that you're not the modern-day 'norm'.

Then there are the two things that most parents struggle to have enough of already – time and money. More children means more demands on both of those finite resources. There are ways around most things though. How much you're willing to compromise or trade off depends on what you really want from life. There is no right or wrong answer to this, just the answer that suits your family unit best.

Holidays can be one of the first things that need a compromise. They can prove not only a hugely expensive luxury but can be downright unappealing when your numbers are big. The luggage, transportation and finding somewhere large enough to accommodate everyone can prove quite the challenge. In recent years we've opted to holiday at home. Renting a house somewhere cuts down on the immediate cost. Houses are usually let at a set price that is not based on the number of people staying there. For once the larger family stands to gain! In addition to this, you can just pack up the car with everything you need, without worrying about airline luggage weight restrictions, and go. The flip side for us has been that my eight-year-old has only very recently been on a plane for the first time. Not a huge deal in the grand scheme of things, but certainly something that I felt guilty about. Then again, as a wise woman said to me, 'You never have to scratch the surface too much to unearth a mother's guilt.'

After-school activities are another huge challenge, both in terms of finances and time. It's impossible to be at the side of two pitches at the one time and there are always other children to be taken care of, even if you and your partner were to try to cover both matches between you. Dance recitals, musical performances, speech and drama exams, and martial arts gradings all place their demands on your evenings and weekends. We try to cut our cloth accordingly here. Everyone can't do everything, so we try to prioritise and overlap were possible. Many after-school activities have progressive discounts for siblings – a huge bonus when your numbers are up. Even better are the ones whose timings also accommodate more than one of your children at the same time.

On a personal level, I like my children to each do something musical or creative and something sporty, but I also like them to have downtime too – time in which they can play their own games with their siblings and friends, using their own imagination and toys in unstructured play.

Time is always in short supply and the demands of raising a large family don't make that any easier. It is really important to try to give each child some of your individual attention to make sure that they don't get lost in the home crowd, and so that you know what's going on with them. As much as possible I try to give each child some 'mammy and me' time, whether it's going out for a hot chocolate and a chat, a trip to the playground, a walk on the beach, or a visit to a friend or cousin with just that child. I try also to take advantage of everyday moments, including the walk home from school and that time just before bed to ask them about the best and worst (if anything) part of their day.

With the bigger age span that often goes hand-in-hand with a larger family, the older children are usually still up when the littles go to bed. My older children love for us all at this stage of the evening to sit down and watch something together, in a phone-free zone.

While undeniably a parent has less time for each individual child as the numbers grow, there is the upside that they have each other and their needs are sometimes met by their siblings. There is usually someone there who can reach the unreachable object, who will help with a difficult-to-open box, or who will even flag concerns that they have over something their sibling has told them. Sometimes they have insights that you as a parent don't. And while the kids love for me to join in with a game they're playing, which I do when I can, that same game will happen with or without me because they have each other and the game's happening is not dependent on me.

One of the big advantages I have found as more siblings have arrived is that the number of arguments between them has actually decreased. I think it might be that they don't get on each other's nerves to the same degree because they can move on and play with someone else if one particular brother or sister is driving them crazy. There is, I suppose though, always the possibility that I just can't hear the arguments these days over the din.

The reality is that there is no magic or perfect number and every permutation and combination brings its own advantages and pitfalls. While having a large family is great, the workload is not for the faint-hearted. I think I am destined to fall into the category of choosing to be done rather than ever feeling it. Love is the drug and having lots of kids feeds the habit.

7

KEEPING IT IN THE FAMILY

Labels are everywhere and everything is subject to them. Parenthood and parenting styles are no exception to the rule. From the pushy and overpowering 'tiger mum' to the more chilled, relaxed, go-with-the-flow 'free-range parent', it appears that everyone must conform to a type, based on their parenting style and ideals. The internet and magazines are full of quizzes whose answers promise to reveal which category you fall into. And as you take the quiz, just for fun of course, you know the answer you're hoping for.

We can all be a little bit guilty of occasionally applying labels, even if not by name, to other mothers. Sometimes it can be because we don't approve of their parenting style. Other times it can be because we feel inferior to their seemingly impeccable high standards.

I'm not convinced that anyone actually parents their children in an exact or exclusive manner. I do believe, however, that our respective parenting styles are influenced by the role and position that each individual child assumes in the family. There's also no denying that we're influenced by our own parents and our own experiences also, whether it's to repeat the pattern that we know or to completely rebel against it. And then there's the majority of us, who'll meet somewhere in the middle.

PARENTING STYLES

In spite of trying my best to be fair to all of my children I have to admit that I don't parent them all the same. I don't think parenting them differently and being fair are mutually exclusive. A variety of personalities in our household means that different children respond in very different ways to motivation and, dare I say it, threats.

There are certain things, however, that I am consistent with. As my children's parent first, rather than their friend, there are times I insist that they do things they don't want to do because I believe it is in their best interests. That can stretch to after-school activities. In the same way that I don't let them miss school on a whim, I rarely say it's OK to skip a scheduled activity of any sort, just because they don't feel like it. Occasions like birthdays, the chance of a playdate or relatives visiting can be valid reasons for giving the activity a miss sometimes – not being bothered isn't.

None of this is because I'm a pushy, driven mum (though I know that some of my more reluctant kung fu attenders might beg to differ), but rather because I want them to appreciate the importance of committing to something. I'm not looking for exceptional achievements from the children, or even insisting that they attend because I paid for it. I just don't want them to get into the habit of giving up on something because they're not bothered. And I would like them to do it to the best of their respective abilities, whatever they may be.

They all have particular activities they really enjoy doing and there are rarely any battles when it comes to their personal favourites. However, if I was to allow them all to just do what they want life might be easier certainly, but they would miss out on the many life and physical skills that some specifically chosen activities offer. Please appreciate that there's no so-called 'tiger mum' forces driving me here. I have neither the finances nor the time to have each child involved in an endless ream of activities. More to the point perhaps, I don't have the inclination either as I think time for free play and just hanging out is really important.

I have several of the children enrolled in martial arts classes. Some are more willing participants than others. One in particular will go to great lengths to avoid it and a suspicion on his part that he is suffering from all manner of tropical diseases and rare, potentially fatal, ailments is not unusual on kung fu day. As much as I love my son with all my heart, I know that he needs a little motivation when it comes to doing anything of a sporty nature. I don't force other sports but I'd like him to be active and this particular activity choice was deliberate because I believed it would help my children with their coordination and focus, and help them to build their core strength. At the same time, their attendance offers me the comfort that one day – a day I hope will never come – if they found themselves in danger they might be able to take care of themselves with the self-defence skills they have learned along the way.

And so they have to go, and there are plenty of children in their class who would much rather be at home, watching cartoons, playing with their electronics or even playing outdoors, but their parents, like me, feel it's a good activity for their children to be involved in. Does that make me a pushy parent? I don't think so. Will they have to do it until the day they turn eighteen? Probably not (unless, of course, by then they want to).

I breastfed my children. They all slept in my bed at some stage. And I believe in immediately responding to your child's needs. I have never left my babies to cry it out and actually feel ill at the mere thought of leaving a child to self-soothe. If my baby cries, I respond immediately. I wouldn't leave one of my older children upset either. To all intents and purposes, I appear to follow the attachment parenting ideology. The reality is that I follow my own ideology.

My children slept in my bed because I was exhausted and this was the best way for me to get some sleep. Co-sleeping wasn't a decision I made, it was more a necessity for survival. I breastfed because I breastfed, and I respond to my children's needs because it's a natural thing to do. After all, who can bear to see their children upset?

But I didn't do any of this because I was following a particular parenting style. In fact the lovely, cosy parenting image that the attachment parenting style evokes can be very much in contrast to the raging lunatic that I have been known, the odd time, to become, when the playroom is turned upside down by a three-year-old who wants to give Spiderman the mission of locating a missing teddy in the carnage he has created, or when I find five pairs of dirty jocks and numerous odd socks wedged down the side of my son's bed. On those particular days I follow the lesser acknowledged, but I believe more frequently practiced, 'losing the plot altogether' parenting style.

Beyond the baby stage, I haven't parented all of my children the same – the reason being they are very different people with very different needs. They need different things from me and how I parent them depends on their personality and the situation. With all of the ups and downs of life, there are certain times when each child needs me more than others.

One size really doesn't fit all when it comes to parenting and no quiz can really tell you the sort of mum you are. As the stages of childhood progress and/or the numbers grow, the only real constant is that you're a mother. Sometimes you'll get it right, sometimes you'll get it wrong, and sometimes a copious amount of chocolate is the only answer.

MULTIPLE PERSONALITIES

Clones of each other are how you might describe my children. Most have similar colouring, most have similar frames and all have sparkly eyes. Physically, they are clones. Each baby who arrived looked more or less the same as the one before, and the one that followed. In fact, some of their baby pictures are almost unidentifiable and the only way I can tell for certain who is who is by looking at what they or the other people in the photograph with them are wearing. With the first few children I was very good about writing their names, the occasion and the date on the back of each photo. As the numbers grew and I evolved to become a 'there's not enough hours in the day' mum, photos of the younger children ended up being printed about a year after they were taken and so the occasion was generally long forgotten. The exception to this is the youngest child; nearly all of his photos are still on my phone.

Looks, of course, can be deceiving however. In spite of appearing as mirror-image babies and, indeed, now as younger and older versions of each other, and in spite of their common undervaluing of sleep as babies, many of them are now as different as chalk and cheese. Their interests are different. Their hobbies are different. Their friends are different and their temperaments are very different. The ingredients may have been the same, but the results certainly are not. So if the essential ingredients are the same, could birth order play a big part in influencing our children's personality?

The Role of Birth Order

The position held by each child in our family has changed over the years, sometimes on several occasions. The only person who has held the same role as successive children have arrived is my daughter, the eldest.

The stereotypes claim that the firstborn is a natural leader, confident and self-assured. The only child is a lonely child, who apparently has difficulty sharing. The ever-babied youngest is carefree and playful and gets away with most things, while the poor old stuck-in-the-middle child has a whole syndrome assigned to them. It makes a lot of sense when you think about it that your older child might assume the role of leader. A confidence comes with experience and your older child has been around longer than their siblings. They are also the only child who ever got to have you to themselves. You will have been their biggest influencer and their main playmate. And, as you played the games correctly and coloured the pictures carefully, they will have mimicked what they saw.

Firstborns typically spend more time in adult company and as a result their vocabulary tends to be more advanced and descriptive. A tall, blonde man might be described as such by a firstborn. A third child, however, will have learned from his older siblings that a more accurate description is 'poo-poo head'.

The arrival of a new baby can be a timely reminder of how far our older child has come in their relatively short life. As we gaze upon this helpless tiny newborn, who cannot even hold their own head, immediately we expect more from our now eldest child. My eldest child stepped up to plate beautifully when her brother was born, and in my eyes suddenly appeared so capable. The truth of the matter is that she was probably ultra-capable for her age, well before his arrival, but the comparison that I could now draw between them made that capability stand out all the more.

When her baby brother was just a few weeks old and she was the grand old age of three, her maturity and capability meant that I could trust her to sit by his side in my bedroom as he slept in his Moses basket. I, in the meantime, was able to take a quick shower in the adjoining ensuite, knowing that she would follow my instructions not to lift him if he woke, but to call me immediately if by some tiny, remote chance I didn't hear him cry.

In contrast, in between writing the last couple of paragraphs I have had to abandon my laptop twice to see to child number six who is currently three years old. He feels none of the weight of responsibility that his sister once did at the same age. He likes to be at one with nature and has yet again been removed from the trampoline where he was bouncing naked while swinging his Hulk costume above his head.

I am the eldest in my family too, so I understand the role and I have always appreciated that my eldest child has assumed, and been given, more responsibility than her younger siblings. What I never quite grasped, before the arrival of several other siblings, was how little she was when we expected so much from her.

Our second child is our eldest boy. He had a brief stint at being both the youngest and the middle child, but he never really fit any of the stereotypes. Cushioned for years from the ultimate expectations of responsibility, our family's larger size means that he now joins his sister in 'the eldest children' category in our house. His chilled (horizontal some might say), agreeable personality has never really changed, in spite of his reassigned positions. He's just too laid back to be bothered by it all and is really still just an older version of his original baby self.

The middle child position in our family has proven to be an ever-moveable feast. And though we have an actual middle child now, who incidentally in no way matches the middle child stereotype – reminding us instead more of his eldest sibling – the large family dynamic means that we probably regard three of our children as the middle children. But while three may hold that position, the three personalities are incredibly different.

I have always believed that child three's experiences after birth were the biggest influence on his personality. He is a much more reserved child than any of his siblings. Having spent a lot of his babyhood and toddlerhood in and out of hospital I believe he learned an element of distrust from his encounters with the lovely doctors and nurses who, just doing their job, smiled and played with him before they stuck a needle in. These days, whenever he is ill he is without a doubt the best patient in the house. He's also the child most likely to remain true to his convictions and not be influenced by the crowd. If he likes something, he likes it. He doesn't care if his peers don't. Whether or not this will still be the case when his teenage years arrive remains to be seen.

Child four is very competitive and focused. He's also very mature and emotionally aware of others for his age. He is the actual middle child and while he doesn't fit the stereotype on so many counts, he is the child most likely of all to protest that 'it's not fair'. Such are the joys of not being allowed to stay up as late as his older siblings, or having the perks associated with being the youngest.

Child five, the last of the middle children, is the self-dubbed favourite child – so no middle child insecurities here. He is a happy child who loves company but is equally content to play alone. He is observant, quirky and a relatively deep thinker for his tender years. He is convinced that he is my favourite child, to the point that it's a joke amongst his siblings. He seems quite willing to accept his role and place in the family without dispute.

The two youngest children are viewed by the older children as the babies of our house. The only children who view child six any differently are child five, because of the close age proximity, and child six himself. Both child six and child seven enjoy many of the advantages of being the youngest and are adored and applauded by their older siblings at every turn. They're also cut a lot of slack by their older brothers and sister, which might explain why my three-year-old is a more adept streaker than watcher of his younger brother.

As the actual baby of the family, child seven is adored by the masses. The other children would literally stand on their heads if they thought it would make him smile or laugh. As a result he is a happy, content little dude, who loves company. Content as he may be though, being child number seven means he's no pushover. He knows exactly how to make himself heard in the crowd.

Recently, three of the older boys went for a sleepover to their nana's house. Child number five was suddenly promoted, temporarily, to the oldest boy in the house. It was a self-realisation that his role had changed and he was very keen to let us know. This was also followed with a claim that he would obviously stay up later that night because he 'was the biggest boy in the house'. But he wasn't just interested in the up-side. He immediately announced that he would prepare breakfast for his little brother. He's only a little dude himself, but he felt he had new responsibilities as a result of his elevated position – responsibilities that he was only too happy to take on. Then again, there was a huge novelty factor at play. It was an eye-opener, though, to the role that birth order plays and the way in which we treat our children depending on their role. Child number five has always been very content in his, but I never realised until then how aware of it he was.

Child six didn't care about being the new 'second biggest boy in the house'. He poured a bottle of baby shampoo down the toilet and flushed it several times.

Although it seems to me that there may well be a small degree of inevitability about the influence of birth order on both the formation of our children's personalities and the manner in which we parent them, there are a few things that we can do to make for a smoother ride.

Parenting the Birth Orders

Parents are often stricter with their firstborn. I'm pretty sure my firstborn would argue that this is in the case in our family anyway and I would certainly claim it was the case when I was growing up.

Your firstborn makes you a first-time parent. Every experience is new, every stage is new and every worry is a first from a parenting perspective. Trying to get the balance right somewhere between encouragement and pushiness, between motivation and pressure, and between keeping them safe and being overprotective, is no mean feat.

Parenting your eldest can feel a little like a game of trial and error, but, as in every situation, trying to see things from their perspective can help to cut down on the rows and ensure that it's not a role of all work and no play:

- Try to give your eldest child a little one-on-one time. A chance to just be your child and not the older sibling of your other children.
- Make sure the advantages of being the eldest child are obvious. A different bedtime, pocket money, permission to do something that the younger children can't – things that distinguish them from their younger siblings in a positive way.
- Cut them a little slack. Being held up as 'the one who should know better' all the time is no fun. Remember that they're still children too, in spite of your frustrations. Hearing comments like this can also build resentment towards their younger siblings, who, to the eldest, can appear not to be held accountable for their actions.
- Manage your expectations so that they can manage theirs. Doing their best, not being the best, is the most important thing, whether that's in school, sports, art or whatever. Precious 'firstborn syndrome', which many of us parents can suffer from, sometimes convinces us that our children are more academic or sportier than they actually are. I've heard it at pitch sides as over-enthusiastic parents roar at their children, confusing under-6 football with a competitive World Cup qualifier. I've witnessed competition on a different level as Junior Infants parents compare school reports, noting with interest whose child scored the most smiley faces. If it appears to your child that being the best always is what matters, you'll stress them out hugely.

Of course it's not all fun and games in the middle either. Yes our middle children don't have to take on the responsibility that their older siblings do, and by the time they come along we're often a little more au fait with this whole parenting business. But middle children rarely get to be the first to do something. They often have to live up to an example set by their older brother or sister, who has had plenty of time to master the goody-two-shoes role without the distraction of siblings. To keep your middle child on track:

- Don't compare. Your middle and eldest children are two completely different people and there is nothing to be gained from reminding your middle child of the sort of things that their older brother or sister would or wouldn't do. It's a one-way ticket to Resentville.
- Make a fuss of their achievements and the occasions in their life. Let the milestones they meet and every birthday party, sports day and school show they have be every bit as big a deal as they were when it was their older sibling's turn. It may not be your first time doing something, but it is theirs.
- Be available to them and make time to talk. Without a later bedtime like their older sibling or the additional time that a younger sibling might need or receive, getting some one-on-one time with you in the natural course of the day might not be easy – so schedule some. And don't wait for there to be an issue of concern before you do it. Schedule it on a regular basis.

And then there's the adored baby of the family, cherished by all – except when some of those cherishers feel aggrieved by the fact that their parents seem to have taken a total leave of their senses, allowing this younger sibling to get away with the sort of thing that would have seen them banned from their iPad or tablet for a month. Parenting them can be an exercise in keeping the entire family on board.

- Be age appropriate. Just because your child is the baby of the family doesn't mean they are an actual baby (unless of course they are and then this point will be totally irrelevant). Encourage independence and let them do age-appropriate things to help in the house. It's also important to make sure they're accountable for their actions in an age-appropriate manner. 'They're only little' can't excuse all actions or misbehaviour. If they are old enough to understand, make sure they understand. You're just storing up trouble for the future otherwise.

- This can't be a double-edged sword. Sometimes the youngest can be left out of things because they're the youngest. The reality is, however, that while they may only be young, having older siblings means they're probably tougher than you think and they can manage to be involved in more than you think too. So try not to mollycoddle and have them miss out.
- Don't take the foot off the pedal too much. Yes, the others might look as if they're turning out half-decent, but there's no room for complacency.
- Be mindful of their needs in all of the commitments you have with your older children. Yes, on the surface it may look as if you have lots of time with your youngest child, but how much of this time is actually quality time and how much is spent on school runs or after-school pick-ups, having lunch in the car in between? Make sure to fit in fun time for them too. It's easy to prioritise the older children's seemingly more important needs, but those of your youngest child are just as important. Do an activity during family time that suits the youngest child best. Let the older children fit in around the youngest for a change.

SIBLING RIVALRY

Nothing is quite as beautiful or as perfect as that moment, after twelve hours of huffing and puffing and panting and pushing and finally squeezing a watermelon out of a nostril-sized hole, when you first set eyes on your precious baby. Well nothing, until you squeeze out baby number one's little brother or sister. And as more watermelons come to join the family, it's easy to find yourself visualising a Walton-esque style scene where everyone just loves Mama, respects

Daddy, plays happily with each other and no one even questions not having the latest Nikes.

Family dynamics don't just change as a new member joins the family, but rather continually evolve as the stages of childhood come and go. Siblings can be lifelong friends, forever confidantes and fierce champions of each other, but along the way they can also be sworn enemies over a coloured cup or a Spiderman mask.

And as your pre-imagined idea of Walton-esque harmony fades rapidly into oblivion with the realisation that your children's favourite pastime is, in fact, knocking the heads off each other rather than cheerfully jumping rope, it can be a shock to the system to note that your kids – the light of your life, the apples of your eye and the centre of your universe – can't seem to stand each other.

Some might argue that there's a case for keeping them separate, and they're probably right at times – especially when tempers are frayed. But let's be honest, part of the reason many of us chose to have more children is so that they would have each other – a lifelong friend and someone with whom they can share their childhood journey. And for anyone who has ever taken a journey, metaphoric or otherwise, there is no denying that a companion you can actually stand is a much preferable option.

We have all manner of personalities in this house. Some gel better than others and some spark off each other with just a look. With a lot of children there are a lot of options and there is an escape in the form of an alternative sibling for those who are finding one or other particularly annoying.

I like to observe my children playing and interacting, and while I don't always pass a comment if I hear a lovely private exchange or conversation take place, primarily for the reason that I don't want them to think 'Big Mother' is always watching, it is one of the nicest things to witness. If I see one sibling assist another with something, or maturely ensure another sibling's safety, I always make a point of commenting. It's an invaluable opportunity to reinforce good, kind and considerate behaviour rather than them only hearing my dulcet fishwife-like tones when they've done something wrong.

What's rare is wonderful of course, and like most families, I imagine (or at the very least hope), breaking up arguments tends to be the flavour of the day most of the time. Even the best buddy siblings row, but there are always those sibling dynamics and relationships that need a little more work than others. Sometimes it's a lack of common interests and other times it too much common interest and too much competition for the same thing. Some siblings feel resentful of other siblings appearing to get all the glory. Others resent having to share their time and space. And then there are the siblings who feel their brother or sister manages to get away with murder.

I try to be pretty mindful of the sibling relationships that might need a little extra work in this house. With certain challenging stages, sibling relationships can be fraught and some stages just involve winding each other up with innocent, but explosion-inducing, teasing all the same. These phases will pass, though you may find yourself saying 'Stop doing this. Stop saying that. I am not a dog. I cannot hear you in that pitch' a lot, while you wait for the said phase to pass, in what seems like perpetual slow motion. Strategic planning when it comes to the positioning of your kids during any car journeys, restaurant braving, family visits or family outings is the best way to cope with this in the interim.

Strategic planning of a different kind can also be useful with children who seem to clash largely because of certain similar personality traits. Every now and then, my children's grandparents ~~are emotionally blackmailed into~~ happily agree to take some of my children for a sleepover. The kids absolutely love this and there is always great excitement in the build-up. There are no chance pairings. Obviously we ~~don't want to discourage the grandparents from ever taking them again~~ want it to be a lovely time for all involved, but sometimes we choose to send two together who could maybe benefit from a little sibling bonding. The kids' grandparents are great and spoil the children rotten when they have them. With trips out, treats and movie nights all enjoyed by a smaller number of children, the environment is conducive to happy thoughts – happy thoughts and no ability to escape to less annoying siblings. There is also the 'away from home' dependence at play. Much as the children love to stay with their grandparents, there is always a little bit of trepidation about the unfamiliar bedtime routine, for example. As children who come from a house where being alone is rarely an option, having a sibling with them when somewhere different, even a sibling who usually drives them crazy, can be a comfort. Amateur psychology at its best perhaps, but it works.

We work on any sibling relationships that might need a little support at home too. One-on-one time is sometimes replaced with one-on-two time and the planning of that 'two' is once again strategic. A trip to the cinema, pizza parlour or muffin shop, or even a shopping trip for the more willing participants, sets the perfect scene. A happy, nice and relaxed experience together often sees the two actually enjoying each other's company, rather than being at loggerheads. It also gives them a chance to chat, really chat, while they're in good form, as opposed to bickering.

There are times when sibling relationships can be strained by the behaviour of one or more siblings. Even if it's not related to a disagreement, sometimes if siblings see another brother or sister displaying challenging behaviour, and appearing to get away with it, it can cause no end of frustration for them. Difficult behaviour from a child in a family doesn't just have an impact on their stressed-out parents, it has a significant and real impact on the other children in the house. No one enjoys the atmosphere that results from the fallout.

It may well be that you have used all of the same discipline and motivating tools you used with your other children but one particular child just doesn't seem to care – or care enough to stop how they're behaving anyway. If you find yourself in this situation, it's in the best interests of the entire family, including the child in question and the relationships between them and their respective siblings, to try to get to the bottom of it and turn things around. If all else has failed, the following might help:

- Change the way in which you say things, even if the meaning is ultimately the same. This might sound like modern-day airy-fairy stuff but it works (tried and tested here). Rather than leading with 'that's it, you're banned from your iPad/tablet/ dessert today', try saying 'if you play nicely with your little brother/help me clean the playroom/tidy your bedroom, etc., you can play on your iPad/tablet/have dessert after dinner later.' The request is still the same. The fallout or gain is still the same. But the manner in which you've put it to your child highlights the advantages of being agreeable to them.

- Whenever you see good behaviour pounce on the opportunity to flag it. Tell your child what you liked about their behaviour and make such a fuss that they're likely to repeat it again.

- It's so easy to do, says she who knows only too well, but don't compare your children. Don't say 'you'd never catch your big brother hiding in the toilet eating his Christmas selection box all in one go.' That's basically pitting one sibling against another. If you want to flag an older sibling's behaviour as something to replicate you should try something like 'it's a good idea to just eat one bar of chocolate today, so that you're not ill and you still have something to look forward to.' Then resist the urge to add through gritted teeth, 'look, look, look, see, HE's sitting over there acting like a normal human being, why can't you?'

- Give your child whose behaviour is proving difficult a chance to explain without going into detonation mode. Try to keep a tab on your own frustrations. Each situation is a new one and while forewarned is forearmed in terms of knowing how your child is likely to react, it's not fair to assume they're immediately guilty of what they have been accused of without hearing the full story. There may well be a reason for their behaviour and yes they shouldn't have pushed another sibling off the (very low) playroom table, and that needs correction, but it may have been in response to having been hit over the head with the dustpan and brush.

- Be fair to your other children and be consistent. This is a part that can prove surprisingly difficult, particularly if you're at the end of your tether with one child and have chosen a 'pick your battles' route. If a normally well-behaved child acts out, be fair to that child and don't over-react. In a subconscious attempt to prove to the child who is usually in trouble that it's not personal and you won't accept bad behaviour from anyone, when it comes to the usually better-behaved child be sure that the punishment fits the crime. This is an especially easy trap to fall into if you've had a long day of battles.

Sibling relationships are unique. They're a link back to a childhood of shared and similar experiences and a continuation of the nuclear family into the future. Siblings are playmates, confidantes, shoulders to cry on, builders of forts, creators of imaginary lands, protectors, teachers, tormentors, cover-uppers, tell-talers, toy grabbers, entertainment providers, carers and sharers of the load.

And the bond lasts. As the rows are forgotten for another day and the dust settles, siblings are there for one another in good times and in bad. The rewards for the parents are clear. It's wonderful to see the love shared, wonderful to see the friendships grow, wonderful to know that they'll always have each other. And it's wonderful to know that in later life, long after the chaos, negotiations and refereeing demands of the childhood years are over, there are a few of them to club together to pay for a decent nursing home or, failing that, to take turns in having you come live with them. Payback time!

8

Time for School

An Ode to Back to School
The new school year is drawing near,
The teachers start to cry,
While parents empty bank accounts,
For school books they must buy,
And uniforms and bags galore,
Shoes and runners are a must,
And pencils, pens and rulers too,
Parents feel that they'll go bust!
There's books to cover,
A lovely task,
And then they'll need a label,
As do the crayons, and lots of pens,
Which adorn the kitchen table.
The hope in labelling every one,
Is that they won't get lost,
That the kids will take good care of them,
After all the mounting cost.
But hopes are not enough I fear,
When it comes to lunchbox lids,
Which disappear in the first few days,
Lost by those pesky kids.
And pencil cases filled to the brim,
At the beginning of September,
By two weeks in, will be quite bare,

Because the kids, they won't remember,
Where they've left their pens and rulers,
Pencils or parers either,
You'll feel your hard work was all in vain,
You'll need to take a breather.
It's the same old drill each and every year,
With a lesson that makes you pensive,
With all the costs when you add it up,
Free education is expensive!

Starting school is a huge milestone in a child's life. It's a huge milestone in their parents' life too, if the truth be known. It can feel as if your child is taking their first step towards independence, and a surrender of some of your control over the amount of access you have to them, timewise, is inevitable. Gone is the freedom of taking your child off for the day as you see fit (assuming you can get the day off work, that is) and in its place are timetables, after-school activities and set school holidays.

Some children take to this new stage in their lives like the proverbial duck to water. Others dig their heels in and resist it all the way, and then there are the children who completely wrong-foot us. The children who are full of smiles, waves and excitement on their first day, enthralled by the whole experience, and caught up in the momentum of it all, only to greet you with a look of horror, somewhere between day two and week two when they realise that this wasn't just a once-off event and they're expected to return every day.

And just like children, parents too can be a mixed bag when it comes to how they feel about their children starting school. Some relish the idea of childfree mornings, or at least 'one down, however many more to go' mornings. Others are overcome with emotion at the mere thought of their child starting school and still can't get their head around where the years have gone. I, unfortunately, fall into the latter category. As many times as I've done it, there's still a part of me that's a little bit broken-hearted every time another one flies the nest – for that four-and-a-half hours. And that little bit of me stays broken-hearted for the first day or two, maybe three even, after which time the novelty of the even shorter two-hour 'adjust-ment/weaning' days has completely worn off and I've taken to ranting about the ridiculousness of the fact that these weaning days are even shorter than the Montessori days and I'm only home from the drop when it's time to collect them again, and did I mention how ridiculous I thought the length of these starting days are?

But the schooldays conundrum starts well before the first day of school even arrives. The question over which school to send them to, how to manage childcare now that there's a school run included and how to juggle work and school holidays can be among the many concerns that parents have. And then there's the age-old perennial favourite: what is the right age to start school?

THE AGE VARIABLE

In every class and every year, someone has to be the eldest and someone has to be the youngest. That's a given, but worrying about whether your child is too young to start or wondering if they'll be bored if you wait an additional year are common concerns.

In Ireland, for children whose birthdays fall at either extreme of the cut-off points it can be a particularly difficult decision. My daughter was the youngest in her class. She started school less than three months after her fourth birthday. She was a tall child who was capable, confident, mature, articulate and extremely sociable. She settled into school incredibly well and her teachers regularly com-mented that it was hard to believe she was the youngest in the class. She made friends easily with her peers, some of whom were more than fifteen months older. She went on playdates and other parents echoed the teachers' comments. She loved the routine of school, absorbed everything she was taught and was the happiest little girl imaginable. In every regard she appeared the perfect candidate for school that September – every regard that is except her age.

If I'm honest, I very much regret our decision to send her to school at the age we did. We can give our children many things. We can help them in many ways. But the one thing we can't do is make them older than they are.

Often, when considering whether or not to start a child at school, a huge amount of emphasis is put on the individual child and the maturity, cognitive abilities and personality of the child in question. These, of course, are essential things to consider, but taking into account the fact that there has been a move towards starting children at school at a later age, I don't think that these factors can stand independent of age, or more precisely the age of your child's potential peer group.

As the years passed, the very few other children in my daughter's class who were close to her in age repeated a year or changed school. As the tween years approached and the teen challenges were visible in the distance, her age began to matter a lot more. I became the mum who seemed to say 'no' to everything. I said 'no' because she was too young – younger than her peers. It's not easy for your child to have to cope with your decision and yet you still have a responsibility to parent them in an age-appropriate manner. The easiest and fairest thing to them is to ensure that they are a similar age to their classmates, because this will be the age group of their peers the entire way through school.

When your child is four or five, it's very difficult to imagine them as a tween or teen encountering all the challenges that age group brings. But the day will come, and a younger child will often have to face and manage the challenges of their older peer group sooner than you would like.

My second child was also very young starting school. With only three years between him and his big sister, I hadn't yet the insight into the challenges that starting school at a young age might bring. Like his sister, he was a sociable, chatty and amenable little dude, but the age span in his class meant that some of the children were seventeen months older than him. That's an enormous difference when you've only been on the planet four short years. We didn't need to wait long though to see the implications of the age difference. By three-quarters of the way through Junior Infants, it was very obvious. As children in his class celebrated their sixth birthdays, my wonderful four-year-old played, sounded and acted like a four-year-old. We decided, with the school, that the best thing would be for him to repeat Junior Infants. It was not an easy decision to make.

On their advice, we took my son out of school for the last week of the final term. This was so he wouldn't be caught up in the preparations of the other children as they moved towards Senior Infants. My son didn't understand what was happening and he wondered why his friends were still at school. The next year was very difficult for him, and even though we knew that we had made the correct decision, it was difficult to watch the impact it had on my little boy. People often say 'they can repeat a year if necessary' as if it's no big deal. Firstly, the option is only there in very particular circumstances and, secondly, it is a very big deal – even in Junior Infants.

The following September, my son entered Junior Infants for the second time. It was a very confusing and unsettling time for him. In spite of repeating the year there were still several children in his class who were older than him, but unlike before they were not significantly older than him. Having already spent a year in school though, the difference between him and the children coming in was noticeable, even the children who were older. They had come straight from Montessori. He had already been conditioned by school rules and routines. Yard time was also difficult for him as he watched his friends from the year previous playing together, but he was not allowed to join in. At my son's school, Junior Infants must play with Junior Infants, Senior Infants with Senior Infants and so forth. My super-chilled little dude was very upset. Things of course did settle down and, to be honest, it's not a period of his life that he even refers to anymore. I'd go so far as to say that he has almost forgotten at this stage that he ever repeated the year. It did, however, take almost the entire school year for him to settle.

Having spoken to other mothers at the school gate whose children also repeated years, I have found their stories to be similar. Repeating a year, if permissible by the school, is not an easy option, even when it's the right one. I have also spoken to several other mums whose children experienced no difficulties, initially, when starting school at a young age. By virtue of a larger age gap between their children, these mums had the ability to see the challenges that faced their children further down the line before having to make a call on the age at which to send their next child to school. Unsurprisingly to me, every parent opted to send their next child at a later age.

Of course, hindsight is a gift we are not blessed with. If it were, we would all be able to get things right and do things perfectly each time. While I have my regrets about the age at which I sent my eldest two children to school, I did what I thought was best at the time. In fairness, that's all any of us can do.

By the time child number three, yet another summer baby, was ready to start school, I had had a little insight into the school system. He is, and was, a totally different personality to his older siblings. His more reserved nature means that I probably would have felt more inclined to wait that extra year anyway, but in light of my experience I was determined. Even if he had been the most sociable child on the planet, in addition to meeting all of the recommended criteria, I had no intention of starting him at school before the age of five.

He didn't happily wave me off on his first day. In fact, he clung to me and announced that he wasn't returning on day two. This was in spite of the fact that he was already five. This was because that's the sort of child he was. As the weeks passed he settled into school well, made friends and enjoyed the whole routine.

As the years have passed I can see that while he's not an overly confident child, he does know what he agrees with and what he doesn't, and he will stick to his guns regardless of what the 'crowd' thinks – a fantastic attribute when navigating the challenges of school life, not so fantastic when you're his mother trying to convince him to sort his room. He's also mature enough to accept that everyone is different and will challenge something he hears from his peers if he believes it unjust or unfair, even if it means going against popular opinion. Peer pressure will always exist. Being older doesn't mean that a child won't be subject to it, but confidence can come with age.

At the same time, my second son has had to cope with his best friend leaving the school and the rejigging of his base class, which means that many of his other friends are no longer in his class. His familiar safety net is gone, and for my home-bird son familiarity is everything. This has been very unsettling for him, as it would be of course for most children, but life doesn't stay the same, and school doesn't stay the same. I'm just grateful that he had the bonus of not having to deal with these challenges and hurdles a year younger.

I have to be honest: I'm not on the fence about this subject. It was flagged to me by my eldest son's school when he first started that he was a little on the young side. I thought I knew best and that it depended on the child, and not on their birthday. The reality is that the current trend towards starting children at school at a later stage means that what was our norm when we were at school, and how we managed, no longer holds the same relevance.

The worry that your child might be too old and may become bored is another common concern. Boredom is easily avoided. There are so many things that you can do with your child yourself, or that your Montessori school/preschool can do to keep your child stimulated. Education need not be solely classroom-based. The best way to get an idea of the age span of the class is to speak with your school principal. The schooldays are about so much more than education. It's best to give your child every advantage you can.

READY FOR SCHOOL

Once you've decided you're going to send your little one to school, it's time to start the preparations. And it's never too early.

- Chatting with your child about school in the months leading up to the first day can build up a sense of anticipation, but if your child has older brothers and sisters you may want to ask them to ease off on their complaints about horrible homework, terrifying teachers and the ultimate fear – a trip to the principal's office.
- Speaking about school in a very positive manner and talking to them about how grown up they will be once they start can all lead to them looking forward to their first day, rather than dreading it.

- If you happen to know any children who are going to be in the same class, organising a few playdates over the summer can be a great way to build confidence in your child regarding the whole experience.
- If, on the other hand, your child is not going to know anyone, don't dwell on it but reassure them that they will make friends very easily.
- Many schools have a welcome day for incoming Junior Infants. Don't miss this if at all possible. These days offer the perfect opportunity to remove a lot of the mystery and possible worry that your child may have about starting. Often your child will get to meet their teacher, as well as seeing their classroom and meeting other children who will be in their class. It can help to calm any fears you may have for your child too. After the welcome day, it's a good idea to chat frequently with your child about their new teacher so that everything stays nice and familiar.
- The school will give guidelines as to the size of schoolbag your son or daughter will need. Once you know this, involve them in shopping for it. Character bags are often popular at this age and while they might not always be as practical as other bags, they're worth a consideration if your child is excited by them. Lunch boxes and beakers need to be such that your child can manage to open them independently. This is something that can be practiced (a lot) ahead of time.
- Save yourself the hassle on a school morning, and your child's teacher throughout the day, and get shoes with Velcro fastening – enough said.
- If your child can't read their name confidently yet, or if the school has a 'school coat', put some marker on the coat somewhere so that they can easily distinguish theirs among a sea of blue, green or black coats at yard and home time. This can be a brightly coloured button sewn to the hood or a distinctive sticker on the sleeve – just something that makes life easier.
- And speaking of coats, make sure they can put it on and take it off themselves. In an effort to speed our children up sometimes, we often do this for them automatically.

- Label everything. Every. Single. Thing. Right down to individual crayons. Chances are several children within the same class will have the same pencil case contents. It's not just cost-saving, it might save you the hassle of replacing them several times over the course of the year.
- The same is true for clothes and uniforms. Four- and five-year-olds don't seem to feel the cold the same way the rest of the world does. When thirty green or red jumpers have been discarded in a pile at yard time, the chances of getting the right one back, first time around, are slim. Hence the real need for the many parent text and social media groups I'm part of, each flooded with daily messages asking if anyone has seen Jim, Mary, Sam, Emma or John Boy's jumper or tracksuit top.
- Revisit toilet hygiene practices with them and make sure they can capably manage their school trousers or skirt, especially if either has a belt.
- Make sure your child can use a tissue or handkerchief without your assistance.

There's plenty of time to practice and prepare for the many things that need doing before the first day of school and other stuff will just fall into place when teacher, who is about to wield more influence than you ever thought possible, sets the rules.

So, with the groundwork done and the seeds of anticipation sown, you and your child are ready to face the first day and weeks that lie ahead. And though there may be stumbling blocks along the way, there is lots you can do to make school days happy days, for one and all.

THE FIRST DAY AT SCHOOL

It's normal for there to be tears on your son or daughter's first day of school. Some of them may even belong to your child. The hype, build-up and nerves peak and the realisation that this is really happening dawns. But it's an exciting day too, and with any luck excitement will be the main focus and feeling of your child.

Most schools have a shorter adjustment period for incoming Junior Infants, and for some that period can go on for a couple of weeks. As the first day arrives, it can be helpful to mention to your child that this is just a short day. It can be comforting for them to realise that whatever their fears, it's not for too long. There are a few things worth bearing in mind that first day:

- On the first day, try to keep your own emotions in check. Children associate tears with sadness and fear. If they see you upset, they're more likely to become upset themselves. Speak positively and excitedly on the way to school, but don't brush off any little concerns your child may mention. Take it as an opportunity to offer more reassurance.
- When you arrive, make sure to point out to your child where the bathroom is and reassure them that it's OK to leave the classroom (once their teacher knows) to use it. This might seem obvious to us, but it can be a real point of concern for small children who are in an unfamiliar place. For a period, some of my children never used the bathroom in school and were always bursting to go at collection time. It also led to a couple of accidents because they were too nervous to ask. Prevention is better than cure. Flag it in advance.
- Don't hang around the classroom too long that morning. It can convince a child that there's something to worry about if they see mum or dad hanging on 'to keep an eye on things'.
- Make sure you, or the person collecting your child, are on time for the pick-up. Being late will just add to their worries at an already emotional and vulnerable time.
- Don't compare your child to older brothers or sisters or even peers. Starting school can be an overwhelming experience and different children react to different situations in their own way.

At the end of the first day, it's natural to be very curious about how those couple of hours went and some children will be only too happy to give you a blow-by-blow account. Other kids, however, will volunteer absolutely nothing. In fact they may even go on to tell you that they did absolutely nothing. If that's the case, rather than push them, make your judgement from their demeanour. Chances are, along with the unquenchable bedtime thirst, you'll get to hear everything later, when they're trying to avoid going to sleep.

BEYOND THE FIRST DAYS

As the days and weeks go by, you'll start to get an indication of your child's true feelings about school. You may also notice a few things that need tweaking – whether it's a necessary earlier bedtime, because school really takes it out of them, or finding a way of making sure their lunchbox doesn't come home as full as it left that morning.

And then there are the parts that we can't completely control – like making new friends. We can help but we can't do it for them. Starting school doesn't just involve lessons for the children; there's a whole new set of lessons for the parents to learn too. Smoothing the transition is an ongoing exercise and the sooner the creases are ironed out, the sooner your child will settle. Standing back and taking stock can be the first lesson in assisting them before moving on and doing our bit.

Establishing a Good Routine

I thought things would be easier when my children started at school. I thought the fact that they were of school age, with a structure to their day, meant that we would automatically fall into a sense of routine. And yes there was a routine of sorts that came naturally, which meant that they went to school at a certain time and came home at a certain time. What I didn't wholly appreciate was how essential it was to create a routine at home to support the new school–life balance.

A set bedtime is a must for schoolchildren. Even if the hours are similar to the hours they might have spent in childcare, the demands are not. Young children are expected to focus at school, unlike their childcare environment where they can move from activity to activity and play as they like. Levels of concentration not required before means that many children who are adjusting to the transition to school often fall asleep in the middle of the afternoon, in spite of it having been a couple of years since an afternoon nap was their norm. Overtired children don't just have more difficulty focusing, they're also more likely to be emotional and get upset easily. Making sure they get sufficient sleep can help to counteract this.

Mornings can be fractious affairs at the best of times and no one likes to start their day with an argument, especially one with their children before they head to school. Organising as much as you can the night before can help to take some of the pressure off an already hectic morning. Leave clothes and underwear out for the next day, including and especially shoes – one always seems to have disappeared off the face of the planet otherwise. Make lunches the night before. Have notes and monies required by the school (numerous times a month it seems) signed and in an envelope ready to go. Have any sports equipment or musical instruments by the door and raincoats at the ready. It's worth getting up earlier yourself too, ahead of the kids, so that you can get ready in peace. You're more likely to feel calm in the midst of the morning storm instead of roaring instructions at your kids with just one leg in your jeans. Resist the urge to hit the snooze button too many times.

Allow yourself plenty of time to arrive at school early. Five minutes can make all the difference in morning traffic and there is a lot to be gained by your child arriving early. Besides feeling less frazzled, lots of schools start the day with free play time. This is a fantastic way for your son or daughter to chat and make new friends while playing with the school toys and using their imagination. It's also a time that most children love – what better way to start the day, especially if your little one has become a reluctant school-goer.

Making Friends

This can be one of the biggest things we as parents worry about, and sometimes it's with good reason. How a child feels about something is often linked to the fun they have, and there's often much more fun to be had when there are friends involved.

It can be of particular concern if your child is a little on the shy side or if they knew nobody in their class prior to starting school. Playdates are one of the buzzwords of the moment now. With parents working, or children going to school a distance from their house, there is no longer the guarantee they will have school friends living close by, or even available to play in the afternoons. Structured playdates have become very much the norm.

Even the shyest of children is generally very open to the idea of a playdate, particularly if it takes place on their territory. Of course if your child doesn't know anyone in their class then there's an excellent chance you don't know any of the parents either. But fear not, there is a way around it – just don your organiser hat, and become the person who arranges the class contact list. It needn't be as intimidating as it sounds. Just have a quick word with the teacher asking her to distribute a brief note introducing yourself, explaining that you're trying to organise a class contact list for ease of contact and list the details you're looking for: name, address, phone number, email, etc. Include your own details for reply and, voila, you've just become the mum whom everyone knows, virtually at least, if not yet necessarily in reality.

Organise a few playdates, but organise them separately. Don't be tempted to have three or four children over at the same time. If you don't know the children already, then you don't know how the dynamics will work. It could be hell. Listen out for names you hear mentioned frequently by your child (for the right reasons) and start there.

Finding Out About Their Day

How much you will find out about your child's day and how it went is down to the sort of questions you pose. 'How was your day?' inevitably produces a 'fine' or 'terrible' answer – 'terrible' generally indicating that teacher gave out to them. 'What did you learn today?' is nicely set up for a 'nothing' reply.

To try to find out a little more, be more pointed with your questions. Focus on letters, sounds and numbers and try asking, 'What letter did you learn about today?' Chances are you'll get a lot more information, or at least enough to ask some more leading questions. One question destined to break the heart of any mother or father is, 'Who were you playing with today?' After many days of being told 'no one' by one of my children, I could stand it no longer and arranged a day's leave from work. I frantically ran down to the school to watch from afar, tissues at the ready, waiting to witness my darling son, ostracised from school society, standing alone on the periphery as all of the other children played together. Funnily enough, that wasn't the scene I happened upon. In the midst of all those children playing together was my laughing boy, happy out and definitely not alone. I asked him again at pick-up time, 'Who were you playing with today, love?' to receive the usual reply – 'no one'. It wasn't that he was looking for sympathy, more that playtime had been over an hour ago. That's a long time in a small child's world. An awful lot can happen in an hour. The real answer was that it was ancient history in his eyes, and he couldn't remember off the top of his head. And before anyone links this to boys – my daughter did the exact same thing.

One thing that can be a little bit more difficult for us as parents to fathom is that sometimes our children want to play alone. It doesn't mean there's anything wrong. It doesn't mean they're lonely or unhappy. It just means that that day their own company was the preferred option. Free to play as they wanted, and free to get lost in their own imagination.

Lunchtime Challenges

I am asked what feels like several hundred times a day, 'What's for lunch/dinner/breakfast/snack/tomorrow's dinner/Friday's dinner?' by a number of children who love their food. Yet in spite of these near insatiable appetites, there were times when their lunchboxes came home almost as full as when they left for school that morning. We have pretty much the same drill here every day regarding what happens when the kids get in from school. They're each told to take their lunchboxes and beakers out of their schoolbags, and after about the fifth time of asking they actually do it. I've become wise enough at this stage to know that any keen emptiers of lunchboxes haven't actually eaten their lunch, hence their sudden cooperative nature, so they're always treated with particular suspicion. I am always told by way of explanation that they 'don't have enough time' to eat their lunch.

I discovered that it was a situation not unique to my household. At every single Junior Infant parents' evening that I have attended, for each of the different children, the same question has been raised by a parent from the class, 'How long do the children get to eat their lunch?'

A visible look of horror has crossed many parents' faces when it was explained that the Junior Infants were in fact getting longer to eat their lunches at that present moment in time to allow for the adjustment to school, but soon the time would be halved. By later classes I have found that this question has stopped, even if the parent grumblings haven't. It's not because parents are no longer having the same issues, but because by this stage they're used to it.

With the schools unlikely to lengthen lunchtimes any time soon, it's up to us as parents to try to provide a lunch that can be managed in the time they do have. Quantity is a good place to start. Be reasonable with the amount given. An oversized lunch can be very off-putting for a child, as well as impractical in terms of time allowance. It's also an excellent opportunity to establish good eating habits in terms of portion size. An appropriately sized lunch gives your child a chance of achieving what you have asked of them and finishing it, rather than feeling defeated before they even start.

Involving your child in lunchtime options is another good idea. Ask them if there is anything in particular that they would like to have for lunch this week? Is that a reasonable option? If it is, great: no excuse not to eat it so. Look for a few different suggestions and give them some of your own. Remind them you are providing what you have discussed so they need to make a special effort to eat it.

If your child has two different breaks, which most schools do, consider wrapping the food for their breaks separately so that it's easily accessible and no time is wasted deciding what to eat (or what not to eat until they have to). Consider also providing a way for your child to store their 'rubbish' from their smaller break in particular. A lot of schools don't allow the children to discard their lunch waste in school so they have to put it back into their bag and bring it home. The smell of fruit cores and empty yoghurt cartons can be very off-putting, especially if, like some of mine had a tendency to do, they place them back in their lunchbox. Nobody feels much like eating the rest of their lunch when their tinfoil is coated in yoghurt. Nappy bags can be a solution here: cheap and compact and usually fragranced to keep school bags from smelling of rotten fruit.

Remind your child the night before, or the morning of school, what they have for lunch that day. This way you can get all the objections out of the way and explain, in advance, exactly why all the reasons they have proposed for not eating their lunch are invalid. It also means they know what to expect so there's no room for disappointment or 'I was hoping for …'.

Good old-fashioned bribery, the secret to good and successful parenting, can be a great tool. If your school allows a small treat on Fridays (lucky you) then talk to your child about what that might be and agree that if they make an extra-special effort to eat their lunch this week that treat might be a possibility. If that's not allowed, maybe a chart recording lunchtime success with a certain amount of ticks by the end of the week/month meriting a favourite magazine/treat or whatever works best for your child.

Above all, be consistent in your expectations and keep the faith. Lunchtime won't always be this type of battle. Unimaginable as it may seem now, the difficulty you will have as they get older is providing enough.

If Things Don't Settle

If the days and weeks go by and your little one is still finding things a struggle and hasn't yet settled as you'd hoped, it may be time to have a word with the teacher. The teacher may be unaware of the difficulties until now and may be able to give you some valuable insight into how things are when you're not there.

Your child's teacher can also be hugely influential when it comes to your child. They can say the exact same thing you have been saying, but it can carry more weight because 'teacher said'. You may well find that with the teacher's gentle persuasion and careful watching, things begin to turn a corner.

***

And so begins the exciting next stage of your child's life. As the first few days and weeks pass and the huge initial adjustment becomes a more familiar norm, the tears, tantrums and worries that may have been will become a distant memory. The adjustment for you, however, may last that little bit longer as you possibly start to appreciate the challenges involved with trying to juggle working outside the home and the many school holidays and closures.

As you begin to live your own life by the school calendar, time seems to pass at a fast and furious rate. Before you know it, Christmas has arrived and the excitement of the first school show beckons. All you need now is a penguin costume ….

9

SCHOOL LIFE

School days, allegedly, are the best days of our lives. Yet if you were to ask any school-going child their opinion the chances are they will vehemently disagree. While plenty of children love school in the early years, somewhere around First Class their enthusiasm seems to wane and dissipate. It's no surprise that these feelings seem to coincide with longer school days and more homework. And the effect is felt by the whole family. With a later collection, homework and after-school activities all spilling into and eating up the afternoons and evenings, school life can have an impact on the entire family.

When midterm breaks come around, I hear some parents complaining and wondering how they're supposed to keep their child occupied for one or two weeks. Yes, it's true that the winter midterms can prove more challenging and, in a country that sees more than its fair share of rain, chucking them outside and locking the door so that they can't get back in isn't really an option. But the freedom from homework and the reclaiming of afternoons for just that brief period of time is so blissful it's almost poetic.

And while schoolchildren might need some convincing that these are actually the best days of their lives and probably won't fully appreciate it until they are older and look back through rose-tinted glasses, which shadow some of the realities that were, schooldays are about so much more than academic lessons. They're about taking those first and progressive steps towards independence of action and thought. They're about negotiating a sea of person-alities and school-yard politics. They're about discovering more about who they are as a person, their strengths and difficulties, and finding their place in the pack. They're about learning to respect the many different types of children they meet. And they're about learning that they too matter and deserve respect and kindness.

For the parents, there's a whole lot of other stuff going on. There's the school-gate politics to get your head around, and the new-age birthday party phenomenon. There's the new ways of doing things, which are very different to how you did them at school. It will lead you sometimes to holding a Third Class Maths book upside down in the hope it might make more sense. At the very least, it will make the same amount of sense.

There's the playdates that grow easier and more complicated at the same time, as family rules and individual boundaries differ as the tween years kick in. There's the whole juggling of working outside the home with school holidays and closures. There's the incessant number of head lice letters that will come home, and have you scratching as you read.

There are the homework battles that leave you drained and frus-trated and the announcement of 'must haves' by tomorrow from your child at 9 p.m. There's the fun of sports days and school shows that let you see your child delight in showing you what they can do, and will fill your heart with pride and your eyes with tears as you watch, overcome with emotion. There's the carefully made artwork, completed without your assistance, but made to tell you how much they love you.

And there are the times that your heart will truly break to see your son or daughter struggle because of the unkindness of another child, perceived or otherwise, or, worse still, bullying behaviour. The school days are indeed a minefield and yet another rollercoaster journey, but with a little bit of guidance and support there's plenty of room for fun too.

HOMEWORK

The Homework Poem

T'was the first day of new term,
A scene that's well known,
On the dining-room table,
The school books were thrown.
The children were wailing,
At the thought of the chore,
While the parents were reminded,
There's nothing they hate more,
Than the prospect of Maths,
And English aplenty,
Spellings 'as Gaeilge',
Learning how to count to twenty.
The stand-off continues,
Much longer than should,
As the troops battled homework,
As hard as they could.
A project is mentioned,
A twist of the knife,
In an afternoon filled
With stresses and strife
And united all parents,
In their heads scream so wild
'I hate homework more now,
Than when I was a child!'

Ah, the joys of homework. That pleasure reserved for when we are all absolutely wrecked after a day's school, work, and having to reassemble the bomb scene left by frantic attempts to get out the door in time for school and/or work that morning. Most parents can relate to the sense of elation felt on those rare occasions that those beautiful five words trip off the tongue of your schoolchild, 'there is no homework tonight.'

What's rare is wonderful of course, so most days we're stuck with the drudgery of homework. Personally I detest it and I can't see the point of it. Children are already exhausted after a long day at school. Having spent hours seated at their desks, focusing and concentrating and learning, the last thing they need when they get home is more time spent doing the same thing. They're tired, you're tired. They're just going through the motions (very slowly) and getting it out of the way.

And then there are the days that strike fear into the hearts of parents everywhere. The days when, usually in addition to homework, a child arrives home with details of a project they have to complete. It's not due for several days often, but for primary school children, not particularly renowned for their strength in time-planning, this makes no difference. If it's not due until next Thursday, then looking at it next Wednesday night will suffice. Hell hath no fury like a child made to do a project (otherwise known as extra homework) before it's due.

More pressure comes with the model that needs to be submitted. Make no mistake, your child's model will up against some pretty stiff competition; so if his homemade Viking long ship resembles a sheep that has just been sheared, you and they will need to up your game. The reality is many of the models are not made by the children. This isn't even my suspicion, which would definitely be aroused, if I didn't already know, having seen some of the displays outside various children's classes. I have actually sat in the company of mums as they painted their impressive creations and solar system displays, and have been the head model for another as she fashioned a Viking helmet for her son.

Be under no illusion, their project is your project, even if (as cruel mum here does) you get them to make their own accompanying models. The younger children will not know how to Google the facts they need. The older children may have difficulty interpreting the facts they find. With both age groups, you'll need to be involved. Chances are, anyway, if you left them unsupervised they'd head straight to YouTube. And so you wonder what the point of it all is.

Mary, John and Sam's mums have already been through school. Do they really need a gold star from the Fourth Class teacher?

All of this work can leave little opportunity for play and, with the time constraints involved, it can put real pressure on the ability to take part in after-school activities. An obesity crisis looms, but there's little time for running around.

However, with homework not looking like it's going anywhere anytime soon, there's nothing to do but make the best of it. A homework routine can really help and who doesn't want more of their evenings back?

- First things first when the kids get home: make sure they have a snack, get changed, use the bathroom, etc., to ensure whatever little opportunities to escape the task at hand that might be proposed by unwilling participants are taken care of in advance.
- Decide prior to beginning who is doing their homework where, before any arguments start. If, like me, you have more children than tables, some of your kids may need to share a homework space. This will need to be a strategic exercise with the ones most bothered by each other's breathing separated. You will know which pairings are likely to result in least distraction and prove to be most productive.
- Make sure the homework area is as clutter-free as possible. A clear desk leads to a clear mind. It also means there are fewer things around to distract a child who is only too willing to be distracted. And it will help you avoid being called twenty times in the space of five minutes to locate a 'missing' Maths book which is just buried beneath the weekend newspapers.
- I have always found that stop-starting homework doesn't really work in this house. Where possible, try to allow for a straight run at the homework. Have a look before the children start at the amount of homework they have, and set a realistic target time for the amount involved. Don't allow your child to go over that. Explain in advance that you will be stopping them after forty-five minutes, one hour or whatever time you have set, and stick to it. Kids can take as long as they're allowed to, especially if

you have daydreamers. Setting the clock gives them a timeframe to work within and gives back a sense of control to the child. It means they will realise that they won't be sitting there doing homework until bedtime. They also won't want to continually go to class the next day without their homework completed, so knowing that you are certain to stop them after a set amount of time can really spur them on.

- Positive reinforcement – we hear this term brandished about all the time, but it can be a very effective tool when trying to encourage your children to get stuck in and get it done properly. Whether it's a comment about how well they are working or the promise of playing outside when they're finished, the carrot definitely works better than the stick here. Even if you feel like banging your head off a wall with frustration about how things are going, try to keep things positive. It can mean the same thing effectively but it's the way you phrase it that matters. 'If you finish that in the next fifteen minutes you can go outside and play with your friends' is much more likely to motivate your child than, 'you're not going out with your friends unless you finish that within the next fifteen minutes.' The second sentence just associates even more negativity with homework.

If, in spite of all of your efforts, homework is really dragging on and leaving your child with no time to enjoy anything else, it may be time to speak with the teacher. You may have concerns that there is too much homework, or contrarily that there isn't very much but it still seems to be taking an age. Either way, the teacher is probably the best person to voice your concerns to. They can offer you guidance on the amount of time the homework should be taking, and give you some advice on how to handle it if the difficulties persist.

There are also the days when, in spite of your best efforts and a reasonable amount of homework, things still go awry and a battle ensues. Don't lose heart; we all have days like that. Stick to the routine and hopefully tomorrow will be a better day.

FRIENDSHIPS

We know that friends are a really important part of our children's school lives. How they feel about school often depends on the friendships they have there. Some children are lucky enough to maintain friendships the entire way through school, while others change friends in line with changing interests and hobbies.

Then there are those whose friends change school or repeat a year, and as a result they suddenly find themselves feeling very insecure about everything. A teacher once advised me that one particular child and his friend were very close. The teacher recommended widening his circle of friends because he had witnessed firsthand how another child in the class was left very unsettled by the sudden departure of his friend to another school. As the teacher quite rightly pointed out, 'you never know what's around the corner.'

It was an easy exercise to widen this particular child's circle. In reality he had lots of friends already; it was just that I had fallen into the habit of reverting to the familiar playdates. Inviting different children over to play was easy, and it certainly meant that my son wasn't quite as put out if his best friend was out sick.

I wish I had had the foresight to do this with another child. My children's school mixes up the classes when the children reach Fourth Class. Personally I'm not a fan of the idea because I think the children have enough upheaval coming with the transition to secondary school. However, this is the school's policy and the children have to adjust. None of my children who have so far been through the reshuffling have taken the change well. It has involved a significant period of adjustment and a period of increased self-consciousness as they felt suddenly subject to the scrutiny of other children who had not been part of their original class. Ten is an age where children seem to become very self-aware. The tween years are underway. In addition to the change, my son's best friend left the school. Worse still, he left the country. My son was traumatised. He still had friends but none of them were as close.

In an age where scheduled playdates seem more the norm than just calling for your friends, the importance of the parents' relationship with other parents cannot be denied. It might well be deemed to fall under the heading of school-gate politics, but knowing other parents is the first step in helping your child to make friends. That's one thing when your children are at the junior end of the school, but as they get older fewer and fewer parents are visible at collection time. Some of the children make their own way home, while other parents wait in parked cars, possibly with sleeping younger siblings.

I have found, by this stage of school, that parents also tend to invest less time in getting to know parents of new students in their children's class, not because they're disinterested but because often their children already have friendships established and the parents have built up a support network in their children's friends' parents – still with me?

Of course playdates are still always an option, the trial and error kind. Sometimes with slightly older children it's a good idea to invite more than one child over at a time. The care element is obviously less as children grow and the group dynamic can work better.

Another thing that's worth a shot when trying to help your slightly older children to make friends is a relatively impromptu Saturday evening party. Invite a few of the names you hear mentioned or, if you don't hear any, go through the class list with your child and get a sense of how they feel about some of the different children.

There is a great novelty about an evening party and it needn't be called a party, just a get-together, to make it sound more informal: pizza, a movie, a game of football, home manicures, whatever is of interest. Something that's easy, uncomplicated and likely to be enjoyed by the troops. Being the host child can help to build your child's self-confidence and the opportunity to hang out with a few of their classmates on a smaller scale can help to build new friendships.

Looking into new after-school activities or hobbies that both hold interest for your child and involve other children in their class is another great way to encourage and assist friendships. Everything holds more appeal if they know someone else there and, if you end up sharing lifts to and from the activity with other parents, it can give the children yet another chance to get to know each other a little better. The reality is parental involvement has more of an impact on our children's social lives than we might realise.

And then there are birthday parties of the new age, much more extravagant type. Gone are the days of a handful of children attending a home birthday party, complete with rice krispie buns and jelly and ice-cream. Nowadays it's play centres, princess- and superhero-themed parties, or cinema and fast food for the especially brave.

The new-aged-style birthday party needn't be feared however, and there's even a way to substantially cut down on the potentially exorbitant costs – share. We share parties with a few other children from the class and it seems to be a very popular concept. Shared parties mean less expense and more hands on duty when birthday party day comes around. It can also allow for the whole class to be invited.

When it comes to sharing, the more the merrier. Five birthday boys have shared a party at the one time in one of my children's classes. As the concept grows, and affordability follows, most of the children in that particular class invite everyone to their party. Another upside for the parents on both sides of the equation is that, regardless of the number of children who are sharing a party, there is a one gift maximum ask. The payback is that your child is also likely to be asked to many birthday parties. It can all help towards developing friendships as well as enjoying their company outside of school.

Younger children are, of course, that little bit easier to assist in the making of friends. As the tween years approach it can be that little bit trickier, particularly when the idea of different rules in different houses really comes into play. And you yourself can find that a familiar feeling starts to rear its head. A feeling you haven't felt since you were in school yourself. A time when standing out was not for the faint-hearted and following the crowd was the easier road. Parental peer pressure is alive and well and it can be just as difficult to resist.

PARENTAL PEER PRESSURE

My kids, like most children their age, love computer games, their tablets, their iPads and their consoles. They have restricted access to all of these things, however, mainly because too much time spent on their electronics turns them into raving lunatics – visibly shaking, buzzing, raving lunatics with heightened emotions to boot. In addition to the restricted time limits, there is also a no electronics in their bedrooms rule. Because of it, I am the worst mum in the world sometimes – I'm learning to live with it.

Of course there are always times when we veer from the rules. Times when we have visitors and when the option of having a cuppa and natter in peace wins always. Times when the kids themselves have friends or cousins visiting and there is a once-off opportunity to play a certain game with someone new. And special occasions, such as birthdays and Christmas holidays, when we turn a blind eye to the clock and spend forty-five minutes calling 'last five minutes, and then it's off.'

Although the time rules can be bendable to allow for the situation, the games rules are non-negotiable. There are certain games banned from this house and which the children have been told they are not allowed to play in their friends' houses either: games of a violent nature, with sexual content and choice language. It's an easy ban to enforce here and I feel justified in my reasons for doing so. I don't want my children to become desensitised to violence or exposed to graphic content at such a young age. Coping with the ban outside of the house, however, is not as easy. With different personalities in the mix, some children are naturally more open to accepting my position on this than others. I am happy to stand my ground however, except for the times when I hear how one of my children isn't invited on a group playdate because if he was to go the host parent wouldn't allow them to play the game. Just like adults, kids can be fickle. I stand my ground nonetheless, but not so contently.

Staying true to yourself is not as easy when someone else has to deal with the consequences of your values, even when you're still confident you are doing the right thing. Telling a child 'no', that they can't go somewhere, do something, play something, wear something or get something is not as easy when 'everyone else' is allowed. Of course 'everyone' isn't, but the truth is enough are.

There has been the flip side too. On one occasion I was considered the ultra-liberal mum in my circles when I allowed my eight-year-old daughter to have her ears pierced. Prior to my breaking from the ranks, there was a rallying of the mother troops and near cries of 'one for all and all for not allowing our daughters to get their ears pierced until secondary school.' I rebelled, but I also hid in my car at school collection time for a period after. And there was a fallout. Other mums broke from the ranks and bowed to the pressure of their daughters who pointed me out as the mum who allowed her daughter to do something they wanted to do. They succumbed to parental peer pressure.

I need to be clear here. I wasn't coaxing anyone to do the same or allow the same as me. I was only interested in what I thought was OK for my daughter – but I started a ball rolling. Now granted, this was a much less serious issue and many of the mums who had a change of heart chatted with me about how they never really knew why they had a particular age in their head in the first place, they just did. And as they saw more and more parents allow their little girls to take this almost rite of passage, they decided that there were more important battles to be fought in life.

Of course it all depends on your perspective and if it matters to you then of course it's worth sticking to your guns. But this one event showed that the herd mentality still exists even in adulthood. If you are struggling and feeling the power and weight of parental peer pressure, direct or unintentional, it's worth trying the following:

- Get your partner on-side and make sure you're both singing from the same hymn sheet.
- Chat with your extended family and ensure you have their support. Even if they don't agree with your thinking, ask them not to vocalise their opinion to or in front of your child. You are the parent after all.
- Chat with your child. Discuss the reasons for your rules and listen to their position. Let them know that you are taking on board their thoughts and feelings but you have to do what you think is best.

- If it might soften the blow, offer an alternative – a playdate relocated to yours, a reviewed timeframe, tweaked or compromised outfit, alternative outing, etc.

And if there is a powerful personality whose attempts at coercion and peer pressure are less than discreet and your resolve, while strong, would prefer not to be publicly challenged, then avoidance is the order of the day. Keep some distance, and if all else fails hide in the car!

AFTER-SCHOOL ACTIVITIES

When my first child started school, I was very open to the idea of giving her every opportunity possible to experience every type of activity possible. The advantages, I believed, outweighed the costs, both financial and time, and so after a morning's work, three separate collections and no lunch, I dragged her two little brothers from A to B to C so that she could try out everything.

While she attended swimming lessons, I battled with buggies, little boys and changing rooms, attempting to wash her hair in the shower afterwards while my toddler tried to join her for a wash, still fully clothed. And while she was at ballet I waited downstairs in the coffee shop with a grumpy, tired baby and a toddler who thought the chairs were there for climbing practice. While she attended piano lessons, I sat in the car with a toddler and a baby who wailed because they couldn't go inside for the lesson with her, and while she was at Irish dancing and French lessons and after-school sports, I hung around outside the school feeding the baby his dinner in the car and reading stories to the toddler. None of this even includes football practice, choir, basketball, and speech and drama, but you can picture the scene. Too much of a good thing very quickly becomes a bad thing.

Maternal guilt can make us do all sorts of weird and quite frankly ridiculous things. Good intentions can do the same. This was a combination of both. I wanted to let her try everything she asked to do, partly because she had to spend some of her school holidays in the crèche and that made me feel terrible, and partly because I wanted to give her every opportunity possible, as I thought it was in her best interests. The result was that I was run ragged, her brothers' lives revolved around their sister, and she was a Jacqueline-of-all-trades, or activities at least, with no significant interest in a lot of them.

By the time it was my eldest son's turn, a lesson had been learned. I had an idea that I wanted them all to try a sport and something musical, and both were open to interpretation. But every single thing was not on the table to try. I wanted my eldest son and the children who followed to try out their chosen activity or activities properly, and I didn't want to spend my afternoons and evenings traipsing around the place, leaving no room for evening downtime.

As the numbers have grown my hand has been forced, and it's made life easier to be honest. In addition to cost, I now factor in timings also. I bend the rules of course if a child really wants to try something and we can work around it, but I try to make sure we work around the whole family and that I'm not a martyr to the cause.

Things to Factor In

- Affordability: some after-school activities offer progressive discounts for siblings. Don't be afraid to ask if it's not obvious.
- Timings: if you have more than one child it may be possible to have the timing of their sessions overlap. Swimming is one such occasion, even if the children are in different groups.
- Enjoyment: yes there are some children who need active encouragement to partake in any after-school activities and giving them an easy out might see them doing absolutely nothing, but for those who are genuinely not enjoying something or who may be involved in team sport, for example, stand back and take stock. Don't make your ambitions their ambitions. As your child gets older, team sports become a lot more competitive. If your son or daughter is not sporty, it might be time to consider a different option for them (another sport even). Children can be cruel and if they feel someone on the team is to blame for a lost match or

a poor performance they're often not backwards about letting them know. Recognise the difference between ability and effort.

- Sharing lifts: this can be a lifesaver and a quality-of-life improver. If one of your children is doing an activity with a friend or classmate, ask the parents if they're interested in sharing an activity run. Everyone stands to benefit if it's done fairly.
- Individual appeal: after-school activities can be a great way for children to explore a side of themselves that doesn't get a huge amount of attention at school. Things like drama, music and dancing can really help to improve a child's confidence as they express themselves in a different way.

Of course, just as important as after-school and extra-curricular activities is free time. Children need time to do absolutely nothing except play, relax and amuse themselves. And parents and families need time too. Modern-day life is more hectic than ever before. Continuing on the never-slowing hamster wheel doesn't do anyone in the household any favours. As a parent you need to create a situation where you have time to enjoy being a parent and enjoy your family. Parenthood is not an endurance test.

Children need to learn how to occupy themselves too. A little bit of boredom never did anyone any harm. There's no need to feel guilty if your child's evenings and weekends are not scheduled to within an inch of their lives. You're not doing them an injustice. You're doing them a favour.

WHEN TROUBLE REARS ITS HEAD

So going back to the cliché we started with, 'schooldays are the happiest days of your life' – except when they aren't. Children can find themselves unhappy at school for all manner of reasons and sometimes there can be a relatively quick fix. A misinterpretation of the teacher, a falling out with friends, a stressful situation in class – all of these things can often be put right by a quick chat with your child and teacher. But, unfortunately, there are also the times when things go much beyond that.

Few things come close to the upset that can be caused to a child who finds themselves the target of others' sneers, jibes, cruelty and physicality. Few things come close to the upset that a parent can feel hearing of their child's subjection to bullying behaviour. It's an emotional situation for all involved and one that needs careful and proactive handling.

All children find themselves falling out with their peers at some stage. Few children will avoid ever having another child say something unkind to them. And lots of children will end up involved in rough play, willing or otherwise. As once-off situations, these scenarios can be dealt with swiftly and effectively. Often the child involved hasn't really realised the hurt their actions have caused. They have hit out verbally or physically in frustration or anger and, while this is still not OK, there is no deliberate targeting.

Bullying behaviour takes a different and much more varied form. The physical is obvious, the emotional less easy to pinpoint. Bullying behaviour at school can include, but is not restricted to, name-calling, rumour-spreading, exclusion, deliberately manipulating games (for example, to have a child always 'on' or never 'on'), mocking, sneering, always having one child the butt of jokes, telling lies about a child, and coercing others to treat a child the same. It's a situation we all hope our child never finds themselves in, but unfortunately for too many it becomes a reality. Bullying can have a detrimental effect on a child's self-esteem and self-worth, so if it's suspected it's really important to act quickly and appropriately.

We had a very difficult situation with one of my children. As a result of prolonged targeting my child's confidence suffered significantly. Mentally, it was a very trying time for him, and for us, his parents, it was heart-breaking to see our son so distraught and anxious. One particularly upsetting incident, which has stayed with me, was made all the worse by his not recognising the situation. He came home from school one day extremely excited by the events of yard time. After months of cruelty, he had been allowed to join in a game played by all of the children, including his chief tormentor. He felt that he had been accepted. A phone call later that evening from a tearful parent revealed that all was not as it seemed. It turned out that once again my son was the butt of the joke. While he thought that the children were playing with him, really the object of the game was to make sure not to catch his 'disease'. Everyone, except my delighted son, knew this. Thankfully, some children were so deeply upset by the game they told their parents. It was the parent of a child who opened up to his mother as he went to bed sobbing who called me. I could understand how the child who witnessed the game felt. My tears wouldn't stop.

It's difficult to remain calm when your child is so unhappy and is being treated so badly and unfairly. It's an emotional time for everyone involved, including the parents of the perpetrators. As hard as it is to do so, try not to let your emotions rule your head. Parenting without emotion is a contradiction in terms, but when it comes to bullying, emotions can cloud our judgement, make us forget important things and possibly not represent our child's interests to the best of our ability. If ever there is a case for parking our emotions, this is it.

My experience of having a child who was bullied in school has taught me this:

- Write it down. Write every incident and date down: what happened, how your child felt and the context. It's very easy to forget otherwise, particularly if you're feeling stressed or upset at a meeting to resolve the issue.
- Don't approach the parents. Nobody will be open to the idea that their child is bullying another child. Go directly to the school teacher or principal. Or, if the bullying is taking place at an after-school activity rather than in school, go to the team coach/dance teacher/activity organiser, etc.
- Prepare for mudslinging. In an ideal world, everyone is rational and accepting of different points of view. We don't live in an ideal world. Attack is the best form of defence and few people are willing to lie down and accept a charge. There can even be shock at what their child is being accused of. Try not to let adverse reactions derail the aim of any meetings.
- Don't leave any meeting with the teacher/principal/activity organiser without a plan of action and a review date, plus a plan

for what to do if things flare up again between then and the review date.

- Don't let your child witness your upset, no matter how hard this is. In the same way that we want to protect our children, our children want to protect us. If they think what they are telling you is upsetting you, they might shy away from telling you more.
- Make sure your child knows that they deserve to be respected and treated fairly and with kindness. The actions of the other child/children are the issue. Your son or daughter is not the issue.
- Know that although the school may take action to stop the behaviour, you may never get the child who is carrying out the bullying behaviour to accept that they have done wrong, and know that their parents may behave similarly. The aim of the meetings with the school is primarily to ensure that the behaviour stops and that your child is in a safe happy environment, where they have the opportunity to thrive rather than cower.
- You are your child's champion. You may not be able to remove what has happened, but you can give them the confidence to know that you will take action to make it stop. Through open conversation you can help your child to recover and to realise that they are spectacular, just as they are. It might be a long road but with your love and support they can get there.

What If Your Child Is Accused of Bullying?

Nobody likes to think or admit that their child might be capable of unkind or bullying behaviour towards another child, and so it's natural if your child is accused of bullying to feel defensive and protective. It's a difficult and sensitive situation but it's important to listen with an open mind and to take stock of what you are told. Stay calm and agree to revert once you have spoken with your child. Later, sit down and discuss the issue with your child in a non-judgemental and listening fashion.

It's also important to remember that your child will give you their perspective on the situation. This may vary wildly from the claims made, or it may support them – either way the situation needs to be dealt with in a calm and practical manner. If your child makes a counter-claim, remain composed and take note of the details so that you can relay them to the school, or activity coach/teacher, in due course.

Talk to your child about the hurt and upset that can be caused by a perceived joke, exclusion or unkind comments or actions. If there has been cause for upset, discuss ways they can make up for their behaviour. Perhaps they can make an apology card for the child who has been hurt.

Parents' acknowledgement of the situation is important too, particularly in the interests of good relations going forward and in setting an example for your child. Reassure the parents of the child who has been upset by events that you are dealing with it and that you will work to make sure there is not a recurrence.

And remember, children are children, looking for guidance from their parents along the right path. Sometimes they make mistakes, just like we as adults do. The important thing is to deal with it, learn from it and steer them back onto the correct course.

***

Primary school is a time filled with fun, friendships, learning and evolving challenges. Once your child starts, it can feel as though life passes by in a whirlwind as you begin to live by the school calendar. Before you know it, your four- or five-year-old whose schoolbag was once almost as big as they is now close on a similar height to you, or may even have taken over. And as they've grown and their time at primary school comes to an end, the next challenge waits. Secondary school is on the horizon, with possibly the biggest changes of all.

10

Adjusting to the Teenage Years

Just when you thought you had it all sussed. Just when you thought you were finally getting the hang of this whole parenting lark and that you might actually have half an idea of what you're doing, you discover you're the parent of a teenager.

Instantly recognisable by their surly disposition and tendency to grunt, teenagers don't generally believe in saying more than is necessary – unless to complain about the injustice of everything in their world. Their world, you understand, not the actual world. The actual world is too busy revolving around them, and if it's not – well then, that's just totally unfair.

The teenage years are yet another minefield for parents and, all joking aside, they're often no walk in the park for a teenager either. It's a time of enormous change, physically and emotionally, and the beginning of the transition to adulthood. For teenagers, hormones wreak havoc in an already challenging time, and for parents living with the fallout – well it can be difficult, to say the least.

As teenagers try to find their place in society it can also be a time of enormous power struggles. Trying to keep their child safe and yet allow them a level of independence can be a difficult balancing act for parents. For the teenager, trying to get their parents to appreciate that they are not babies anymore can be an uphill struggle. With two sides sometimes pulling in opposite directions, the scene is set perfectly for the mother of all battles.

We were all teenagers ourselves. We all thought the world didn't understand us and that we were going to change it for the better with our open and free-living attitude. We remember that stage probably better than any other of our childhoods, and the angst, fun and, let's be honest, mischief involved. And yet in spite of all our clear recollections, we don't seem to be much better equipped to deal with these years when our children arrive there. It still remains one of the most challenging stages of parenthood.

Things are different now. Technology has evolved to a level that means teenagers are never away from the influence of their peers. Their lives are lived out online – the highs and the lows and the bits they may one day regret sharing. Teenagers don't come home from school, close the front door and 'park' the day's conversations with friends. Our conversations with friends and peers in the evening time, after school, may have been a quick phone call as our mothers roared at us to 'get off the phone' and ask what could we possibly have to talk about as we'd been with them all day. These days the conversations with friends and peers continue well after school ends, infiltrating family life as mobile phones, an extension of the teenager's arm, ping all through dinner time and evening time and bedtime, if it's allowed.

So the struggle for balance continues. A balance made all the more difficult by the ever-present peer influence. So much happens during the teenage years that pinning it all down to a chapter is nigh on impossible, but some of the typical issues and shocks to the system that you might encounter are covered here.

'What doesn't kill you makes you stronger' it is alleged. Consider the teenage years your heavyweight training.

THE MOVE TO SECONDARY SCHOOL

One of the first big changes that a teenager and their parents often have to navigate is the transition to secondary school. The move often involves saying goodbye to a group of classmates, together since the age of four or five, as children head to different schools. Sometimes it's a much anticipated change. Some kids look forward to the new challenges and feel they're ready to leave behind the 'babyish' primary school. Looking at the older teenagers, they long to be part of a cooler gang of older kids. Other children are more apprehensive, preferring what is familiar and worried about how they will cope in their new surroundings.

Regardless of which camp your child finds themself in, one of the biggest shocks to their system will be finding that they are bottom of the pile again. Having been the oldest in the school at primary, it can be quite the reality check to find themselves viewed as the babies of the school once more.

Preparing your child for secondary school is not too dissimilar to preparing them for primary. Most schools host open days or evenings and these are great opportunities to let your son or daughter have a look around what will be their new surroundings. Seeing the different classes, lockers and facilities can help them to visualise, a little at least, the different structure that will make up their day.

Having an open chat with your child can give you the opportunity to respond to any concerns they may have. You might not have all the answers but you can talk about how you may get them. If your child is not going to a school that most of their friends are going to, they can be worried about being alone. The reality is that schools often bring first years in on a separate day to the rest of the school, which gives them a chance to mingle without the intimidating presence of the older years. Often schools have varied sports and other types of clubs that they encourage first years to join, which will not only help them to make new friends but can also help them to get the best out of their whole school experience.

Timetables are an adjustment, one for which little preparation can be done. It's worth reminding your new secondary school child about the importance of looking at their timetable each night to make sure they have the correct books with them each day and to encourage them to make use of their locker so that they're not carting heavy books around with them unnecessarily.

Homework will be another adjustment, and the assignment of homework that is not due until several days later can take a lot of getting used to. In the early days and weeks, until they get into the swing of things, be the voice in their ear reminding them not to leave it all until the night before it's due, because they never know what other homework is coming down the line.

It's not just the students who find the change to secondary school a challenge. Very unlike their first day at primary school, not every new secondary school student wants their parents there on the first day. It's a big event in their lives and a big marker in ours. It's easy to feel a bit pushed out as their mum and dad but it's the beginning of us not being cool enough anymore, I'm afraid. And this is just a taster.

Another part that can be difficult for parents to adjust to is the comparative lack of involvement you may feel. The teachers will tend to deal with the children directly for a lot of things, and why not: they're old enough to understand. While our signature may be required on permission slips still, gone are the days of notes arriving home about absolutely everything. There will be contact about bigger things, of course, but the day-to-day equipment/material needs and changes will often just be directed through your child, so you'll need to actively and frequently ask.

While living by the school calendar became a norm when our children started primary school, the shorter secondary school year means that the years seem to go by even faster. Secondary school doesn't just bring about a change in how our children are educated, but it's often the place where the friendships develop that influence how those teenage years play out.

THE ROLE OF PEERS

The pre-teen years may have flagged the involuntary metamorphosis that was taking place in your role as a parent, but the teen years will leave you in no doubt. Where once you wielded great influence, and your thoughts and feelings with regards to so much were possibly even replicated by your child, now the arrival of all-knowing and much cooler peers means you're regarded as 'just not having a clue'.

As frustrating a situation as this can be, it's really important not to let it drive you to the levels of distraction that mean you move away from keeping the lines of communication open. That is more important now than ever, as the influence of peers can affect the choices your teen makes with regards to many of the temptations you may be fearful of.

Friends are an important part of a teenager's life and solid friendships can help them to feel better about themselves, and give you the comfort of knowing they are with someone who will look out for them when they're out and about. But friendships can also be a cause for concern too, particularly if your son or daughter is especially impressionable. Recognising their importance to your teen without surrendering your own influence can be a delicate operation.

Loosening the apron strings is especially difficult the first time around, but it needs to be done a bit. Keeping too tight a hold on the reins means your teen will just feel frustrated, especially if they haven't given you reason to distrust them. To feel a little bit more confident about it, lay down some ground rules and stick to them. Don't be dissuaded by the rules of other parents. Chances are, if they're volunteered to you by your teen it's on a selective basis anyway. Some things that might help are:

- If your son or daughter is going out (and yes they will want to go to that disco you swore you would never allow them to go to, and you will reconsider it if all of their peers are going, because you won't want them to feel left out), check which friends are going with them. If you don't already have the parents' phone number ask for it. Explain that it is so you can arrange a lift share. It can of course be for that, but it's also handy to have it for double-checking arrangements (a little bit sneaky, but what harm?).
- The first time, suggest that your son or daughter gets ready in your house. That way you'll get to see the outfits, if that's a concern, and make sure that no drink is involved before they leave the house. If you have daughters prepare to not recognise your bathroom after the preparations of several teenage girls at once and invest in a mask to filter the make-up and tan dust particles that will fill the air for days to follow, never mind the

perfume droplets. Teenage girls are very messy; for some reason this seems to be a shock to dads who are often under the illusion that messiness is reserved for the male of the species.

- Pick your battles. There is a certain look that needs to be accomplished. For boys at the younger end of the teenage spectrum that look is the 'just walked off the football pitch look'; in fact it may well actually be the 'just walked off the football pitch outfit'. For girls the look often involves outfits more suited to a strip club, with skin that glows a certain shade of tangerine. You and your teen will not fully agree on an outfit and, to be honest, they won't overly care what you think unless you like it – and then they'll be convinced there's something wrong with it. Of course you won't like it, because the outfit will look as if all that's missing is a pole. The best thing to do is compromise and meet somewhere in the middle. And as for the tangerine glow, it'll wear off eventually. Just stick to dark bedsheets in the interim.
- Have a serious chat before friends arrive about the rules regarding alcohol, cigarettes, drugs, boys/girls, etc. Explain to your teen that you are trusting them and that they are going out on the strength of this trust. Remind them to keep an eye on their drink and, most importantly, remind them that they can call you at any time, even if they just feel uncomfortable or worried. Explain that it won't mean they can't go again, because they'll have made the correct choice and mature decision.
- Do the pick-up yourself. It'll give you an idea of what really happens at the disco.

It's important that your teen knows they can trust you and can speak with you about what's really going on in their circles. Try not to appear too shocked by anything you hear in the aftermath of a disco, or just day-to-day teenage life. You don't want your teen clamming up and not sharing with you again going forward.

And do not use it against them. If they mention that a good friend was drunk, in spite of only being thirteen or fourteen, bear it in mind in terms of how responsible they can be for each other on a night out going forward, and make your decisions privately, but never tell your teen that they can't go out with that person in the future because they might get drunk again. You'll just give your teen a reason not to place their trust in you and trust is so important at this stage of life.

While trust is everything, bear in mind that your teen will only tell you what they want you to know; other stuff you might just find out by chance, or not at all. It's worth considering an agreement with parents of your teen's peers whereby you alert each other to things that you think might be of concern to them. Of course sometimes there'll be no truth to it (such as the time I was told that my daughter had had her tongue pierced at thirteen – she hadn't), but sometimes there will. It's essential if you go down this road not to shoot the messenger. All we have is each other to rely on during these sometimes turbulent years.

Peer Pressure Fallout

Peer pressure can, of course, encourage our teens to engage in things we don't want them to, and that's made all the more difficult if our teenager's core friend group are already doing them. While the temptation as parents can be to criticise friends who are engaging in the activities we are attempting to encourage our own teens to resist, that approach is likely to backfire. It's better to focus on discussing with your teen how they needn't follow suit and the fallout that can occur as a result of drinking, smoking, taking drugs or having sex at too young an age.

It can also be a good idea to encourage your teen to widen their group of friends through common interests or hobbies. It gives your teen another outlet if peer pressure is proving too much, and it stops the potential risks and fallout of the all-eggs-in-one-basket approach.

It's also a good idea to speak with your teen about an approach they can take if they're feeling the pressure to do, or engage in, something they are not comfortable with. Maybe it could be a text to you, to have you come to collect them, or a made-up excuse that protects them from embarrassment, but lets them leave where they are. Either way, they should be able to seek your assistance without the fear of repercussion.

With the advent of social media and its ever-growing use, teens can rarely escape the influence of their peers. So teaching them about online safety and knowing when to seek your support is just as important as recognising when to do so in the non-virtual world.

THE SOCIAL MEDIA OBSESSION

When my eldest child was still in primary school, all talk was about what age she would get a phone. I was told about countless other children who already had phones but I had a set idea about the age that was appropriate, and even necessary, and believed that I was keeping her safe through my refusal to purchase one.

Now I realise that any child with an electronic device can potentially be placed in the same danger as a youngster with a phone. Teenagers nowadays often don't text through their network, preferring to correspond through social media applications over the internet. The phone is just smaller and more portable. It's available for calls if necessary. It's rarely used for such.

The dominance of social media in our teenagers' lives means not only is it difficult to escape the influence of their peers but there is ongoing judgement, always. Photos shared online look for validation from strangers, and literal strangers they often are, as the competition grows to see who has the most 'friends'. We can and should remind our teenagers about the importance of only being 'virtual' friends with people they actually really know and have met in real life. Trying to ensure that remains the case is a different story however, as is knowing when snooping becomes a violation of privacy. There are mixed views on whether or not a parent should check their teenager's phone. While it may well be an invasion of their privacy when they're an older teen, as a younger teen, much more unfamiliar with the dangers that online life can bring, sometimes it's about putting safety ahead of privacy.

One of the conditions of my older children getting phones was that I could do a spot check on them at any time. It wasn't about micro-managing their online activity or friendships but about ensuring that they were safe. I was very glad I did this when, shortly after my eldest began secondary school, I realised that it was very popular amongst the children in her year to follow what only can be described as 'dark' sites. Thankfully, it wasn't because anything involved affected her, or any of her friends as turned out, but because these were 'cool' sites to follow and the bonus was that they offered a follow for a follow – a real appeal for teens who are all about numbers. A quick chat with the parents of some of her peers alerted other horrified mothers to the fact that their teens were also following the same sites.

There was a double danger here. The 'coolness' of the sites meant that it was difficult for any parent to ascertain whether or not their teen was struggling mentally or emotionally. The other was the imagery and philosophies that the teenagers were exposed to on a daily basis. It was a darker side of the internet that preyed on vulnerable and impressionable minds.

Of course staying on top of things is no mean feat when teenagers are the social media whizz kids, rather than parents. You can follow them on every social media platform possible but, unless you are equally as advanced as they, they can block you, set up other accounts or prevent you from seeing things they don't want you to see. Spying and stalking won't get you far as a parent and, after all, the teenage years are supposed to be about preparing for adulthood. Chatting with them about responsible social media use and online activity is the better option. To help your teenager to use social media responsibly and to stay safe online:

- Ensure your teenager uses appropriate privacy settings.
- Set ground rules.
- Consider a no phone/electronics in the bedroom rule.
- Limit the amount of phone time as you might iPad/tablet time.
- Speak with them about the dangers of social media and online forums, including cyberbullying, and how people can present false identities online.

- Remind them that what they post is there forever – potentially to be viewed by a future employer.
- Talk to them about the need to behave responsibly and respectfully when engaging with others online.

Social media can be a fun way for teenagers to communicate with their friends and is a very real part of modern teenage life, but, like everything, it is open to abuse and exploitation. Being aware of their online activity can help you to keep them safe, but preparing them and reminding them of your availability if they have any concerns or worries is even more important.

Communication remains the key to surviving the teenage years – communication that may well have to be driven by you.

KEEPING THE LINES OF COMMUNICATION OPEN

There was a time when your child hung on your every word and followed you everywhere, including the bathroom, unable to bear being apart from you for even a few seconds. There was a time when all your child sought from you was your approval, and that approval meant everything because you were the super-coolest person in the whole world.

There was a time when your child was proud that you were their mum or dad and they loved to be seen in public with you, and could even be witnessed telling you they loved you without batting as much as an eyelid. And there was time your question 'How was your day love?' wouldn't be misconstrued as you taking a pop at them.

Ah, those were the days. The days before you suddenly became a person likely to come out with all sorts of embarrassing things, things that could cause your newly minted teenager to wish the ground would open up and swallow them in front of their super-cool friends. Things like 'ah, hiya Mary.'

Now, nobody understands them. The world is against them. And their brother breathing is purely done to annoy them.

Living with a teenager is sometimes not easy, and their unpredictable mood swings and new-found belief that you don't know anything can make it all the more difficult. Even though we know it's a period of life dictated by hormones, it can still be pretty hard to take. And as some teenagers retreat to their rooms and withdraw from family life to a degree, the temptation to leave them to it in the interests of family serenity is really there. It's not an option though. Keeping the lines of communication open is one of the most important things you can do as the parent of a teen, and it's essential to continue the efforts in spite of any attempted resistance.

Ways to Improve Communication

- Spend time together. Don't allow your teenager to take up residence in their room, appearing only at dinnertime or when they need washing done. Have set family mealtimes where everyone can sit and chat about their day. But in addition to this, spend individual time with your teen and build on your relationship. Go for coffee, a walk, a bite to eat – something that you can do together, just the two of you. Chat about what's going on in their lives and ask about their friends. Make this a regular thing rather than a once-off.
- Listen. Actually listen and don't just talk. It can be hard to say nothing if you're shocked by some of the things your teen tells you, but you can't let on – and don't roll your eyes. By listening you're not only getting some insight into their lives, you're also allowing your teenager to be heard. They know you are interested in what they have to say and in what their opinions are, even if you don't agree with them. If you listen without freaking out, no matter how much you feel like doing so, your teenager is more likely to give you the opportunity to listen again.
- Take a real interest in their interests. It'll give you a common ground for conversation and show your teen that you value what's important to them.
- Be approachable in every regard. Let your teen know through your actions and words that you won't lose your head as a result

of what they tell you. Let them know if they're ever in trouble that they can speak with you and you will work it out together. Don't assume they know – tell them. Be approachable with requests. That doesn't mean you have to say yes all of the time, but you don't have to say no all of the time either. Know what's important to you. Pick your battles, and when something isn't completely off the wall or unreasonable consider it. If you're the parent who says no to every single thing they are asked, you might not always be asked.

- Try to start conversations on a positive note. If you entered your teenager's room prior to their arrival home from school there is an excellent chance that the mess you encountered has left you fit to spontaneously combust. The danger is that that combusting might happen as soon as your teen walks in the door. Take a breath and start with something like, 'Would you like a cup of tea/glass of juice/hot chocolate love?' Chat about how school went and then move to saying, 'Would you run up and sort your room quickly before dinner is ready please?' The saying 'you catch more flies with honey than vinegar' applies to teenagers too – plus you've managed to avoid another row.
- Don't waste your time trying to sort anything or have a discussion if neither of you is calm. It's a one-way ticket to a full-on row where nothing gets resolved and chances are the situation will end up even worse as things are said in the heat of the moment. If one or other of you is wound up, walk away and come back to the discussion when you have both calmed down.
- And then, there's the leading by example. If you want your teen to be calm, stay calm yourself. If you don't want your teen to shout at you, don't shout at them. And if you want them to acknowledge when they've done something wrong and apologise, make sure you practice what you preach. Raising teens is an emotive experience. No one manages to keep their cool all of the time; you'll have your opportunity to show them what you expect.

The teen years present more challenges than probably any other stage of parenthood. And it's probably the most unpredictable of stages as no one can pinpoint the difficulties or hurdles that may come any individual teen's way. With so many more influences than just the nuclear family at play, there are many more variables to take into account, and it's impossible to predict which influence and variable will play the biggest role.

Effectively, the teenage years mean you're dealing with soon-to-be adults. Soon-to-be adults who want to discover the world for themselves and whose natural inclination is to break away a little from us. Their view is very much in contrast with our natural urge to protect our babies. But our job as parents goes beyond just protecting our children. They are our babies, toddlers, children, tweens and teenagers for a short time in the grand scheme of things. Our role is to help them to develop as a person, ready to face the big, bad world without us – and hopefully appreciate the need to wear clean underwear.

***

Parenthood is tough and it's not for the faint-hearted but it's not an endurance test either. It's an epic journey, filled with highs and lows and overflowing with tears, love and laughter. It's a real voyage to be undertaken by real people and, as we know, many have survived parenthood and lived to tell the tale. The important part in the midst of the madness, chaos and mayhem is to remember to enjoy it too.